Enlightenment

The Keys To Consciousness

Martyn Wilson

ISBN: 978-1-326-48133-9

PublishNation
www.publishnation.co.uk

Contents

Foreword

First and foremost I am by no means a writer. That much will become abundantly clear as you work your way through these pages. The important thing is to concentrate on the message rather than the writing style or my extremely loose grasp of the written English language. Enlightenment is a very simple concept that needs very few words to explain what it is to those who have already experienced it. In fact, If this book were to only ever be seen by those who have awakened, every page would be blank. Unfortunately the rest of the population requires a more detailed explanation with many more words. I have tried to keep the word count to a minimum whilst making sure to cover all of the important aspects of the subject before us. At around 35,000 words I have managed to keep the word count well below the average for a non-fiction title (50,000), but above William Shakespeare's Hamlet (30,557 words). Now thats an achievement! Not that I am comparing my work to that of William Shakespeare, although I will be raising some really important questions (to be or not be is not one of them) with the potential to offer life changing answers.

'The Keys to Consciousness' is written with the sole purpose of sharing my own personal experiences. It is not meant to offend or challenge anyone else's beliefs or experiences, whether cultural, religious or otherwise. It is an account of my personal experiences with a view to helping others experience and understand a similar state of being. I cannot ever know what others have experienced because I have not seen their experiences through my own eyes, and by the same token, no one can ever truly know what I have experienced because again, they cannot see my life through their eyes.

I do not consider myself to be religious, spiritual, a guru, a sage or a leader. I am open to all possibilities and accepting of other people's beliefs and opinions. That doesn't mean that I agree or disagree with them; it just means that I accept their viewpoint. I accept that they have and believe in their opinion. I share my experiences to allow others to look at their opinions and to think about what they are basing their opinions on. Most opinions and beliefs are based on hearsay rather than actual life experience. Many beliefs and opinions cannot be proved or disproved one way or the other and yet people argue and fight to protect their opinion. The acceptance of Enlightenment takes away the need to protect an opinion, the need to argue and fight. Enlightenment empowers you to just accept personal beliefs for exactly what they are: opinions.

I think it is important from the outset to point out that being Enlightened, Self-Realised, Conscious, or whatever you want to call it, is not necessarily an absolute must for everyone. I don't believe there is a right path that everyone must follow. I believe that I have been given a gift that has completely changed my life. I also believe that it would be a waste of this gift not to share what I have learned and experienced, not because I am on some spiritual mission to convert the entire population of Earth, but to point out that there is another way of living, another choice.

I observe people and situations in a much clearer way than I ever did before. I see peoples behaviours and their self destructive ways so clearly now and have noticed that most people have no idea that they have a choice not to act in a certain way. They have no idea that their daily stress is self induced and can be prevented. They see situations as happening to them rather than happening around them. They allow everyday situations to become a personal attack to the point where life becomes a burden. Life is for living, not for suffering. A few simple choices can completely turn a life around. A new way of thinking can transform every situation from a negative into a positive. So, this book is not intended to preach to you how you should live your life, but to offer you more life choices.

How will you choose to live your life?

You can spend
your entire life
trying to be at
one with everything,
or a single moment
realising that
you already are.

Chapter 1

Who Am I?

Who is Martyn Wilson? That really is the ultimate question. It would be too easy to just say that I am Martyn Wilson. Most people, when asked the same question, would also give their name as an answer; after all, that is what we have always been told right from birth. Our identity and our name have become one and the same, but is that really who we are, or are we something much deeper than just a name? This is food for thought and something for you to think about before we journey through this book.

I was born in 1970 in the South of England to working class parents. I had a pretty normal upbringing with no major dramas along the way. We were neither rich nor poor; just average. I have never been religious, spiritual or intuitive. I never really enjoyed school and always looked forward to the day when I could leave and start work. I was part of a gang that bullied anyone who we deemed inferior to us. I didn't sit any exams and therefore never attended college. I drifted from one dead end job to another until I lost count of how many jobs I had actually held, but one thing that I was absolutely certain of was that the next job was the one that would make me happy, and the next one, and the next. The problem was that none of them made me happy. Neither did the next car or the next house or the next holiday. This same pattern continued for many years and left in its wake a lot of heart aches, broken dreams and failed relationships.

In 2002, I found myself in a situation as a single parent bringing up my three small children. This is when I met the person without whom I am not sure I would be where I am today. Actually I had met Maria, a single parent from my boy's school, a few years earlier as Maria's daughter and my youngest son had attended the nursery class together. There had always been a silent connection between us but I was married and so we never really spoke to one another. A few years on and now single, I reconnected with Maria via the School's

PTA while helping out at the Summer Fair, and two years later we were married.

Maria had been a legal secretary for many years prior to having her daughter, and therefore was well educated and well spoken, unlike myself. By the time we started dating, Maria had retrained and started practicing as a holistic therapist and continues to advance her knowledge via training courses, books, videos and seminars. It's safe to say that I have always had Maria on a pedestal and have been in awe of her vast knowledge and superior vocabulary, but I never really understood any of it. I guess at times I felt inferior and would constantly challenge and question anything she had learned. I now understand that it was my ego mind fearing rejection from Maria who was becoming so knowledgeable that she would soon no longer need me. A few years ago, Maria attempted to introduce me to the concept of Enlightenment which I challenged as fiercely as I had previously done so with her other theories and teachings. I found the whole concept absolutely ridiculous and wondered how anyone could believe such nonsense—especially the highly intelligent Maria!

My job at that time allowed me a great deal of free time during the day, home alone while the rest of the family were at work, school and college. I began researching Spiritual Enlightenment and the so called Gurus and teachers that Maria had mentioned. I even went along to a weekend seminar with one of these Gurus. The reason for my research was not to gain an understanding or to obtain Enlightenment, but to discount and disprove its very existence and to discredit the Gurus and teachers that were spreading it. I really was the most unlikely person to ever understand any of this stuff and I was on a mission to show Maria how wrong she was. Now, here's the problem. Somewhere along the way I started to get it. I started to understand what Maria had been trying to tell me for many years. The more I researched, the more I realised how wrong I had been. I started to read countless books on the subject. I watched hundreds of hours of videos. I practiced many different methods of reaching a state of no thought, just to see if any of them actually worked. Once I found a method that worked, I practiced it. The more I practiced the better I got. At first it would last for just a few seconds, but then as time went on I was managing this state of no thought for minutes at a time, then hours, then days, then weeks and months, until my mind fell silent without me trying anymore. This was the first time that I could remember not actually thinking about anything and just being still. At this point I didn't know what to say to Maria. Although this state of no thought is far from Enlightenment, it was a state that Maria had been striving towards for many years. How could I tell her that I had the very thing that she wanted without going through the years of training that she had? I tried to keep it quiet but it was apparent to anyone close to me that something had changed and so I eventually had to tell Maria what I was experiencing.

Maria struggled to understand it and it caused a great deal of friction between us. I didn't want to upset her but at the same time, I knew that this was the stillness and happiness I had been searching for over the course of many years without even realising that I had been searching. I was no longer trying to achieve anything or prove anything and was simply enjoying living in the moment. All thoughts and emotions of the past and future were gone and I was extremely happy. Maria once asked me if it was like someone had switched a light on. I answered that it was more like someone had switched the light off. Everything was peaceful and still and I began to look at the world through fresh eyes in a non-judgemental, non-prejudiced way. I was more accepting of other people's beliefs, more compassionate and more understanding. My attitude changed and my temper subsided. I felt free for the first time in my life.

I can remember wondering if this was it, Enlightenment; but surely if I was wondering about it, it couldn't actually be it, could it? After many weeks and months of being in this space, I began to notice some changes within me. I struggled with bright colours and lights. I found loud noises, music and TV unbearable. I became really sensitive and emotional to the point where I could be watching a YouTube video and just suddenly burst into tears. I was crying at films that never used to affect me, TV adverts that weren't particularly sad, and Facebook quotes that I used to laugh at and call pathetic. What the hell was happening to me? Was I turning into a big sissy girl? (no offence meant, girls. Sorry :)) After a few weeks I settled into this new phase and the light and sound sensitivity went away, but the emotional part stayed. Was this Enlightenment? The fact that I was still asking the question gave me my answer.

At this point, I knew I wanted to help other people but was not really sure how. I looked at various ways but finally settled on Life Coaching. I attended courses in London alongside a home study course and eventually became a qualified Life Coach. I also became attuned to Reiki to the Master / Teacher level. I began practicing as a Life Coach and became intrigued with people and their emotions and problems. I learned how to read body language, eye movement, facial expressions and speech to unravel the causes of mental and emotional problems, but something was still missing: intuition. As I said earlier, I have never been intuitive. Maria had always talked about intuition with her clients and I had always assumed that intuition appeared as a clear picture in the mind of exactly what was needed. I then realised that intuition was much more subtle and I had to really know how to read the signs that appeared constantly before me. This was a fun phase to go through and once I knew what to look for, my intuition began to flow freely. Was this Enlightenment? Again, the answer was in the question.

The next phase was by far the most powerful, coming into the heart centre. An overwhelming feeling of energy radiating out from the solar plexus area of the body. I used to place Maria's hand on my chest and ask if she could feel the energy as it felt so strong and powerful it was hard to believe that it could not be felt on the outside. With this energy came a sense of oneness with everything, a feeling of being a part of everyone and everything. I now know that everything is energy, every person, every animal, every tree, every plant, every object is all made of the same thing: energy. And so we are all connected to everyone and everything, but knowing it and experiencing it are two completely different things (or one completely connected thing!) It took some months to get used to this phase and to settle into it, but once I had settled in, I thought I was there. I thought the journey was over. Was this Enlightenment? Oh crap, I asked the question again! Living in the moment is truly awesome. Living from the heart centre is a magical experience. Being intuitive is a gift. Surrendering to what is rather than fighting against life is an amazing experience. Being emotionally detached from the past and future is a Godsend, but none of these things are Enlightenment. Enlightenment is the knowing that follows. The true acceptance of who you really are deep down in the very core of your being. Enter the final phase, the phase that no longer has a need for questions or answers because it just is, and this is where I find myself. So who am I? Martyn Wilson is just the label given to this flesh puppet, this vessel that I travel in. I am not a name, I am not this body, I am not my past, I am not my actions. I am something far more complex yet something far more simple than what you see. I just am.

*If you hear people talk
about me, people that I may
have known in the past,
they speak of someone
they no longer know,
someone that no
longer exists.*

*Don't judge me
by my past;
I no longer
live there.*

Chapter 2

Am I Enlightened?

Am I Enlightened? This is a question that I have been asked on a number of occasions. To answer such a question, one must first ask many other questions such as: what is Enlightenment? What is your interpretation of the word? Do any two Enlightened individuals experience the same thing? The term 'Enlightenment' can mean many different things to many different people. It translates into many different words, meanings and understandings in various cultures and religions all around the world. Some believe that to reach true Enlightenment one must ascend from this mortal body to a higher plane. Some believe that Enlightenment is reached during this Human existence through meditation, prayer or chanting.

To me Enlightenment is just another word that holds no great power. I prefer to use other words that equally hold no great power, such as Awareness, Consciousness and Self-Realisation. This is just a personal preference, but if you choose or prefer the word Enlightenment, then that's absolutely fine. To me, they all mean the same thing—but to you, they may not. For the sake of clarity I'll explain what these words mean to me. Enlightenment is not merely being in a state of no uncontrolled thoughts entering your mind; it is far deeper than this. It's the realisation that you have a choice whether or not to suffer life. An acceptance of everything that is. An openness to all possibilities. The dissolution of emotional attachment to past and future, and a deep knowing that everything is one and we are everything. Easy!

It has often been assumed that the word Enlightenment originates from Buddhist traditions, an assumption that is flawed due to the fact that Buddhism is over 2500 years old and the word Enlightenment has only been around for about 300 years. The first use of the word Enlightenment or The Enlightenment, is thought to have been a description of a new intellectual movement of the seventeenth century, which promoted the powers of human reason through science, religious tolerance, and the forming of honest governments.

Over the years, the word Enlightenment has been borrowed to translate Buddhist terms such as Bodhi (meaning Awakening), Nirvana (meaning to let go of disturbing emotions and desires) and full Buddhahood (meaning the attainment of self-realisation as exemplified by Siddhartha Gautama, also known as the Buddha). The word Enlightenment has also been used to translate words such as Moksha (meaning Liberation) in Hinduism. In simple terms, the word Enlightenment when used in a spiritual sense refers to the full comprehension of being present or awake. My path has led me to this very state of being that is described as Spiritually Enlightened. So, in this sense of the word, I am happy to say that I am Enlightened.

I have been challenged with many questions designed to trip me up or spark an angry or emotional reaction from me. I have been told that what I am experiencing is not Enlightenment and I totally accept that opinion. Its strange how people get so angry and try to disprove everything I am saying, but doesn't that sound familiar? It's the same situation that led me to where I am today. My experiences stemmed from my trying to disprove Enlightenment, so just maybe those people who attack me are on the right path to Enlightenment themselves. I cannot argue with their opinion because I cannot prove or disprove what I have experienced. I know what I have experienced but there is no way of showing that to others. Ultimately, it doesn't matter whether people choose to believe me or not because it doesn't change who I am. Its an argument that cannot be won or lost, an argument that has no point, and that's an argument not worth having. And so I simply accept their opinions as opinions and quietly carry on with my life.

I have met others who claim to be Enlightened but none of them have experienced exactly the same things I have. Some of their experiences are similar to my own and some of their experiences are very different. I can only take their word for what they have experienced and take them at face value but I can never truly know what they have experienced. I accept their opinions but I also accept that there are other possibilities, and I also accept that I am in exactly the same situation. It's a situation that makes it very difficult to measure yourself against another to arrive at a definite conclusion.

Enlightenment seems to be a very individual experience rather than a shared experience.

This chapter started with the question 'Am I Enlightened?'. From my experiences and from my understanding of the word, I feel comfortable to say that I am Enlightened, but this of course is only my opinion or belief. Your opinion or belief may differ from mine and that is absolutely fine. So what is the truth? Am I Enlightened? Who knows? Who cares? After all, it's only a word.

*Silence is not as
quiet as you may think.
Silence is something
you can hear if you
allow yourself to listen.*

Chapter 3

I Don't Know

To be able to say 'I don't know' is the most liberating thing I have ever spoken. I can remember way back before I knew anything about Awareness, if I had been asked a question that I did not know the answer to, my ego would kick in and make up an answer so as to not appear weak or stupid. I never thought of it as lying as the answer I gave was always based on something I had heard or read or had a vague memory of, topped up and exaggerated to make it sound believable. If you truly observe your own behaviour you will find an element of this within yourself. I am not saying that you are being consciously dishonest, just that the ego mind is very powerful and will do anything and everything not to show weakness. In a state of ego mind, to say 'I don't know' is difficult, and even if you are able to do it, you will tend to beat yourself up for not knowing and will carry that feeling forward into the future.

It's amazing how we tell one another that most of what we read in the newspapers is rubbish, and yet when we read the published word we believe it. People's lives have been destroyed by a few words printed in a newspaper. Published words have turned mere mortals into superheroes, idiots into experts, and genuine people into villains. The pen really is mightier than the sword (although I wouldn't fancy going into a sword fight armed with just a pen!). Now stop and think how many times you have answered a question based on something you have read in a newspaper, book or magazine. You believed your answer because you had read it, and yet just because it was published does not make it true. The same can be said for television; just because it is on the screen it does not make it true. Most of the answers we give are based on what we have read, seen on TV or heard third hand from a friend. These answers are, at best, just opinions, not fact. So why do we defend the answers we give so intensely? Quite simply, it's the power of the ego mind.

Once you can let go of the ego mind you realise that there is no shame in not knowing everything. It is not important if you do not possess all of the answers. When you are asked a question, take some time to consider whether or not your answer is one hundred percent fact. For example, if you are asked if you can rub your tummy and pat yourself on the head at the same time (we have all tried this at some point), you can try it and then give an absolute answer, yes or no. If you are asked if there is an alternate universe on the other side of a black hole then you cannot answer because you do not know, nobody knows. Now before you bombard me with emails and links to the million and one books and videos on the subject of black holes, no one has actually, physically travelled through a black hole, seen what was on the other side, taken pictures, videos and samples and then brought back the evidence. Anything written on the subject is theory not fact. By the same token, no one can disprove the theories. So if your answer cannot be proved or disproved one way or the other, you need to drop the answer and admit that you do not know. Without the ego mind you will have no emotional attachment to whether you know the answer or not.

I was recently asked if my state of Awareness was there forever. This is a great question in many different ways. My belief is that everything is energy and that energy never dies, so even when this body dies the energy that controlled it will live on. I'm not necessarily talking about reincarnation as I have no idea whether the energy will remain as it is now and move to another being or whether it will separate and move on to lots of different living things. I just believe that the energy will live on in some form. Of course this body will not live forever and this state of Awareness may not last as long as this body. I don't know if it is here to stay or if it will be gone tomorrow. It's not something that troubles me or keeps me awake at night. I accept that I have been given a gift and I enjoy it every moment I have it. This is one of a million questions that I do not know the answer to. I like to think that I will continue to enjoy this Awareness until my dying day but I will not know if it will last that long until that day comes.

I am very aware that others seeking Enlightenment look to me for answers. Many believe that to be Enlightened means to have the key to universal knowledge and the answers to every question.

Unfortunately, this is not true in my experience. If anything I would say that I have fewer answers than before but the ones I do have are honest answers. The human race has very few absolute answers. Most answers are again hearsay, opinion, belief, theory and lies. The honest answer to a lot of questions is 'I don't know'. The look of disappointment when I say 'I don't know' is fascinating. Human nature hates 'I don't know'. The ego mind hates not having an answer because it believes that to not know the answer will display weakness, and yet if you are honest with yourself and not controlled by ego, 'I don't know' is the most powerful words you can use. Try it for yourself.

*You can forgive
yourself for not
knowing something
that you didn't know
before you learned it.*

Chapter 4

Is Enlightenment Our Natural State?

One of the most interesting and intriguing questions I have been asked is if Enlightenment is in fact our natural state. To clarify the question, are we born into this world, into this life as Enlightened beings? I cannot give a definite answer to this question because to be absolutely honest, I just don't know. I can give an opinion based on my own experiences. As I said at the beginning of the book, Enlightenment and it's meaning are a matter of personal opinion. To me Enlightenment is the acceptance of all that is, a total surrender and a letting go of all belief systems, a mind and soul clear of uncontrolled thoughts produced by the ego mind, living life in the present moment, and self Awareness of who we really are. I suppose the question should be, does a child possess all of these things before being influenced and programmed by society, culture, religion, adults and life in general?

There have been numerous studies into child psychology and behaviour science with a wide range of results. We know that from birth to about the age of seven or eight, a child's mind is not consumed with the uncontrolled thoughts, social conditioning and belief systems that plague adulthood. A child's mind is very different from the ego mind of an adult. A child sees things very differently, a lot more simply, uncomplicated, and in most cases in plain black and white. This is not to say that a child thinks logically or comes up with the best or safest answers. It just means that they see things in much simpler terms because they have not learnt life's lessons. A child will play games and create and build things just because it feels good to do so, rather than for status, monetary gain or power.

From the age of about seven or eight, a child begins to form his or her own opinions based on their surroundings, upbringing and schooling. Their ego mind begins to form. They are literally a sponge for knowledge. A lot of what they see on TV or read in the newspapers may not be true, but they will take it on board anyway, which then forms the basis of their own belief systems. They are literally screwed up by life. But were they Enlightened beings before we screwed them up? I think we can probably agree that a child lives life in the present moment, as they have no awareness to the past and future. They have not yet formed belief systems, so they will therefore have an acceptance to everything just the way it is. They will have no uncontrolled thought as they have no knowledge of anything yet. So the final piece of the puzzle is, do they have an awareness of who they really are? Maybe, maybe not, I guess we will never truly know.

Another question arises: If we did not screw kids up by passing on our beliefs, teachings and social conditioning, would they grow up Enlightened? My own personal opinion is that the unlearning of what we thought we knew, the letting go and surrendering is all part of the process to Enlightenment. When I look back on my own life and especially at the negative aspects of it, it would be very easy to have regrets and a wish to be able to go back and make changes. A few years ago, I probably would have done just that had I been given the opportunity, but now things are very different. I now realise that those negative aspects of my life were not negatives at all but life lessons that paved the way to get me to where I am today. Without those life lessons, I would most definitely not have found myself in the position I find myself in today. That's not to say that I would not have found Enlightenment anyway. I guess I'll never know if that is the case but I believe that I would probably have been a different person or a different character. To look at life in this manner deletes all regrets and takes positives out of even the most negative situations.

My own personal opinion is that children will form their own opinions and belief systems no matter how we choose to bring them up. I don't believe Enlightenment can be programmed into a child and no matter what we do as adults, they will inevitably form their own outlook on life and create their own ego mind as they grow into adulthood. It would be great to be proved wrong on this subject and be given a new way of parenting that would produce Enlightened children. I won't hold my breath, though, as I think that Enlightenment involves a personal process of letting go and acceptance. Without life's baggage, there would be nothing to let go of and nothing to accept.

I think that maybe a child has a deep level of awareness before life takes hold and that living in the moment is part and parcel of early childhood, but I am not convinced that this is Enlightenment and therefore it is difficult for me to believe that Enlightenment is our natural state.

Maybe it is our natural state, but Enlightenment cannot be experienced fully until we have experienced the contrast of the ego mind. I guess it is just another question to add to the pile of 'I don't knows.'

*Enlightenment is
remembering who
you were before
you were told who
you should be.*

Chapter 5

No Thought

A state of no thought or mindfulness should not be confused with never thinking. Thinking is an important part of life and a very useful tool for planning, problem solving, working and socialising. So what is meant by mindfulness? Mindfulness is the total escape from uncontrolled thought. Uncontrolled thoughts enter your mind uninvited and take control of your very being. Uncontrolled thoughts, also known as the ego mind, are always negative and bring with them negative emotions that create stress in the mind and body. Controlled thoughts are those thoughts that you choose to think and are almost always positive.

It is a common misconception that mindfulness and Enlightenment are the same thing. Mindfulness is an important aspect of Enlightenment but Enlightenment is something much deeper. The process that led me to where I am today started with mastering the art of mindfulness and from my own personal experience I would say that uncontrolled thought is no more than a habit. Just like any other habit it is a learned behaviour that is so deeply programmed into our very being that it can be very difficult to separate ourselves from it. The habit becomes a part of us but just like any other habit it can be broken. The only way to break any habit is to replace it with another habit, a better habit. In this case, it would be swapping the habit of uncontrolled thought for the habit of no uncontrolled thought. Later on in the book, we will look at the process to Enlightenment and also some tools to help break the habit of uncontrolled thought.

Being in a state of no uncontrolled thought can be very difficult to achieve, being as uncontrolled thought has ruled your life since childhood. It can be the most debilitating habit you will ever possess and will constantly throw you into doubt and disarray in every area of life. The more you allow the ego mind to fill your head with uncontrolled thoughts, the more stress and uncertainty you will place on your life. The ego mind grows in power with every uncontrolled thought your brain processes. The ego mind, although just a part of your mind, is almost like a separate entity living inside of you that has taken over your thought processes.

The ego mind fears annihilation and will therefore do anything it can to prevent you from taking away the most powerful weapon in its arsenal, uncontrolled thought. The ego mind is an expert at playing mind games and its only mission in life is to keep you in a constant state of fear. It achieves this through uncontrolled thought to create negative emotions such as worry, jealousy, anger, anxiety, depression, guilt, sadness and disappointment. Some would say that these emotions are just a natural and normal part of life, and to a certain extent they are, but what most people do not realise is that negative emotions release certain hormones into the bloodstream that can seriously damage your health and even be fatal. This level of stress on the body is neither natural nor normal, and living in a constant state of stress will deprive you of the life you deserve.

Controlled thought is very different as you are in control to think whatever you want to. You can of course still choose to think negative thoughts if you wish to but why would you? Why would you choose to think negative thoughts that will start the chain reaction of negative emotions, stress, illness and possibly an early death? I am sure that given the opportunity you would choose positive thoughts. Controlled thought is essential for planning your life and problem solving and is probably the most powerful tool you have. You use it each and every day of the week at home, work and in social situations. You use it in conversation, explanation and when asking or answering questions. The problem is that this awesome tool's power is reduced by negative uncontrolled thought. Your problem solving ability is seriously reduced by the ego mind. Your questions and answers become negative and your explanations are flawed.

Try to imagine how powerful your mind could be if it was not clouded by negative uncontrolled thought. Your questions and answers are not swayed by negative emotions. Your explanations will be clearly thought out and not produced from a place of stress. Your opinions are considered before they are spoken, and your life planning becomes a smooth ride rather than the roller-coaster that has become so familiar. When I finally realised that my life had been dominated by uncontrolled thought and ruled by the ego mind, I found a way to overcome the negative thinking and emotions. The biggest change for me was that once the negative thought patterns had stopped I realised that I actually had very little to say. I used to be able to talk people's ears off. I was extremely opinionated, full of useless information and suggestions on how others should live their lives and never really looked at just how screwed up my own life was. I now quietly observe others doing the self same thing and I find it fascinating because they do not know that they have a choice. Before reading this, did you realise that you had a choice, a way out of uncontrolled thought? You do now! So will you choose to continue with your self destructive thought patterns or will you choose to overcome the ego mind and start thinking for yourself?

The ultimate freedom is the freedom from your own mind.

Chapter 6

Mindfulness

I have been asked on more than one occasion to describe the process that one must go through to reach Enlightenment. I'm not sure there is any one process that works for everyone, a 'one size fits all' solution to an age old problem. I can tell you the process that I went through and maybe this can be used as a guide to find the solution on your own path to Enlightenment. The same can be said for any spiritual teacher, they can only teach their own truth. Your truth may be very different from theirs, but then it may be exactly the same. The important thing is not to get too wrapped up in any one teacher or any one process. To be Enlightened is to be open and accepting of all possibilities. Rigidity promotes thoughts and emotions that will keep you in a state of ego mind.

My path or my truth was to first quiet my mind of thought, and this step alone is the subject of debate. Some might say that to quiet the mind will then dissolve negative emotions and thus solve the problems of life. Others might say that if you face your problems, the emotions will dissolve and thus still the mind. I can't say which is correct or if they are both correct, I can only tell you that for me it was a quieting of the mind that led to the dissolving of emotion and thus the solving of problems. Many people struggle to reach this point as the ego mind can sometimes be too overpowering for them to regain control of their thoughts. Others may find this step easy and I suppose it all depends on your current state of mind and unique set of circumstances. Reaching this point is a huge step and a huge wow factor, but it is not Enlightenment.

Uncontrolled thought, also referred to as the ego mind, has been created by your upbringing and experiences, translated by your own internal filters based on your belief systems and social conditioning. Now, that is quite a mess to unravel! To simplify it, the uncontrolled thoughts entering your mind are based on fear of events from the past and future. Logically thinking, the past has already gone and cannot be changed and the future hasn't happened yet, so why worry?

Unfortunately the ego mind thrives on fear and will use every trick in the book to stop you from destroying it. This is why it can appear so difficult for many people to escape the ego mind. One of the biggest mistakes made by seekers of Awareness is to try to stop these thoughts, as the ego mind will naturally defend its position as a survival instinct. The key is to embrace the thoughts and observe them. Don't try to analyse them or make sense of them, but simply be aware and observe them. You may think that you already do this, but do you really? If uncontrolled thought has become a part of your normal everyday life, as it has for most of the world's population, then this is not observed.

So, how do you observe your thoughts? Well, meditation seems to be the preferred route of the gurus and masters of the Spiritual World. That said, I have met people who have been meditating for many years with no real clue as to how to, or why they are doing it! I have researched many forms of meditation including silent and guided meditations, and to be honest I became more and more confused as to what meditation actually was. The conclusion I reached was that it was simply a refocusing of the mind away from the ego mind. This is all well and good and will give you a break from the ego mind, but many forms of meditation take you so far away from your thoughts that you are unable to observe them. Some might say that this is a good thing, but from my truth, the observation of the ego mind was necessary to dissolve the negative thoughts. The complete blocking of thoughts was a temporary relief but never lasted, no matter how long I practiced.

For me, the solution came via one very simple tool, which, in fairness, could also be labelled as a form of meditation, although I have never really considered it to be so. I can't even remember where I found this technique but it is something I have passed on to others and it has also worked for them. The technique involves picturing yourself in a room standing in front of a fish tank. It is important to see yourself and the fish tank, because you are now the observer of both. While visualising, take any thoughts you have at that moment and put them in the fish tank. Now just watch them. Do not attempt to understand them or to analyse them, just watch them. They may float, they may sink, they may swim around, but no matter what they do, just watch, observe. Now ask yourself a simple question, 'What will my next thought be?'. If you are observing your thoughts without analysis, there will be no answer to the question, only silence. You will feel a very deep and satisfying stillness that you have probably not experienced before. Now all you have to do is rewind, repeat, and do it again, a few thousand times. Simple!

This technique worked immediately for me but only lasted a second or two before the ego mind took control again, but that second or two of deep silence gave me a glimpse of where I knew I had to be. So I did it again, and again, and again, over and over, all day everyday, and because it was visualised in my mind, I was able to keep on doing it whether I was at home or at work, anytime of night or day. The more I practiced the technique the longer the silence became. After quite some time the seconds turned into minutes, then hours, then days and then weeks.

At this stage, I should point out to you a down side that I discovered. Hopefully this is only my experience and something unique to my path, but after long periods of silence when the ego mind crept back in, I would find myself in a very low, depressive mood. I have never suffered with anxiety or depression and I can only pretend to understand how it feels, but these moods came for no apparent reason. Nothing had gone wrong or upset me and yet I felt as if I had the weight of the world on my shoulders. This dark mood was too powerful to allow me to practice the fish tank technique and I had to wait it out until I could find the strength to brush myself off and get back to the silence. This mood would last for maybe a day at the most, and then I would get straight back to the technique and carry on. The people around me noticed a massive difference in my mood swings, loving the highs but hating the lows. I have always been a positive person and like most people, I had good days and bad days. But I was now having more good days than bad, and I mean really good days. The lows were worth it if it meant going for long periods of time in such a buoyant mood. As the months went by, the fish tank technique was being used less and less as the silence lasted longer and longer. I was now going months at a time without any uncontrolled thoughts disturbing the silence. The lows became less frequent and lasted for less time than before, until one day I realised that I could not remember the last time I had had a low or used the fish tank technique. I was in complete control of my thoughts. All emotional attachment to the past and future were gone.

To view this first step from my experience or my truth, I would have to say that whatever method, technique or meditation you choose to use, make sure that you focus on observing your thoughts rather than trying to block them out. Embrace your thoughts and be aware of them without analysing them or trying to understand them.

It's important not to get confused with the ego mind and the thinking mind. The ego mind produces uncontrolled negative thoughts. The thinking mind is a tool to be used for positive controlled thought. Thinking is how we get things done and plan our lives. I now think what I want to think about, when I want to think about it. When I don't want to think, my mind is silent. It's an awesome place to be but it is only a stepping stone to the bigger picture, Enlightenment.

Worrying will never take
away tomorrow's troubles,
just as regret will never
erase yesterday's mistakes.

Worry and regret will only
remove today's peace.

Chapter 7

Beliefs and Opinions

The second part of the process for me was the dissolving of all belief systems and social conditioning. I personally found this not to be too great of a challenge and there could be a couple of reasons for this. Firstly, I had already conquered my ego mind and so the ego played no part in this next step. Secondly, I had never been spiritual or religious and had been reasonably open minded to various possibilities before any of this happened. I admit that I used to question and research everything I heard rather than just accepting it. I believed that to question was to grow, and this still holds true for the path to Enlightenment. Self-Realisation is all about looking into and questioning ones self to discover who we really are. Once we realise who we are, our own truth, there will be no more questions.

The world is full of opinions, belief systems and social conditioning that cannot be proved or disproved either way, and yet people argue and fight battles to defend their position every single day. The ego mind plays a massive part in this, so if you can overcome the power of the ego mind first, you will be in a much better position to dissolve the belief systems and conditionings that have built up in you for many years.

What do we mean by belief systems and social conditioning? Well, If you take the mind of a child, it is pure and unpolluted until we, the adults, teach them and begin to fill their minds with information based on our own beliefs, experiences and social environment. The child's mind will mix this information with their own experiences to form what will eventually become their own beliefs and opinions. As the child grows up they will of course experience new things, learn new things, read newspapers, watch the news, listen to gossip and form new beliefs and opinions. But the problem is that most of this information cannot be proved or disproved either way, it is just beliefs and opinions. The Buddha is reported to have said 'People with opinions just go around bothering one another', and that is very true. One person will give an opinion, the next person has a different opinion, and then the ego mind will jump in to defend its position even though neither one of you can prove that you are right. That's just human nature, or maybe that's just another belief system! I've heard it said that everything is a belief system, and that statement in itself is also a belief system.

Once you quiet the ego mind and remove the emotional attachment to the past and future, you will be well equipped to dissolve all of your belief systems and social conditioning just by simply observing them and questioning them. This self enquiry is a real eye opener to your behaviour. To be the witness of your own behaviour and to experience the realisation that comes with it is quite a revelation. To dissolve your own beliefs is simply a case of self observation.

The next time you are involved in a deep and meaningful conversation, be aware of what you are about to say. Think about your words before you speak. Ask yourself if what you are about to say is fact or opinion. Is there any evidence to back up what you are preaching? Can your words be proved or disproved one way or the other? If you can prove what you are saying and back up your words with factual evidence then by all means, carry on. If you cannot prove or disprove what you are about to say then say nothing. Be brave enough to admit and to say that you do not know. There is absolutely no point whatsoever in having an argument over a subject that cannot be backed up or proved either way. It will only lead to conflicts of opinions, disagreements, arguments, fights, loss of friendships and relationships, bad feeling, stress, anxiety and all other kinds of emotional trauma. None of these things is worth going through just because your ego mind wants to be right.

Another word of caution that you may want to consider is to carefully consider your opinion before you speak, even if you know that your opinion is one hundred percent correct and can be backed up with factual evidence. Is your opinion going to upset the person you are speaking to or hurt their feelings? Do you really want to upset them or dent their ego? Their ego will no doubt defend its position and fight back, creating an argument. Sometimes it is far better to keep your opinion to yourself to prevent hurting feelings and creating arguments. I was brought up to believe that honesty is always the best policy, but now I know that sometimes silence is the best policy.

*When you stop
thinking and believing,
everything will be ok.
A mind closed by
beliefs can be opened
by acceptance.*

Chapter 8

Surrender

The third part of the puzzle is Surrender. After silencing my mind and dissolving my belief systems, the next stage was about letting go, an acceptance of everything just the way it was. This stage unravelled all by itself without any effort on my part. All feeling seemed to move from my head to my heart centre. I no longer felt a need to change anyone or anything. I had no more stress in my body. There was no more need to argue a point or prove that I was right. Material things became irrelevant and money became just another tool to use in my human experience. It's important to point out that there is nothing wrong with money. I still work and I still earn money. I still eat, pay the bills and buy clothes. I still run a car and go on holidays. All of these things require money. I have heard it said that money is the root of all evil, but that is a fear created by the ego mind to keep you in fear and to keep the ego mind alive. Money is just another tool and although it is a requirement to maintain my current lifestyle, I no longer crave riches, recognition, status or possessions. Just remember that the likes of Jesus and Buddha still had to eat and buy clothes. They still had a requirement for either money or a means of payment for the basics. No matter how Enlightened they became, they still lived a human life with human requirements.

It is this part of the process that I have struggled to explain to others the most. Everyone seems to get the first two phases of silencing the mind of uncontrolled thought and the dissolving of beliefs, but this third part, surrender, is more difficult to explain purely because it raises the question of how. How does one surrender? As I have already said, I did nothing, it just happened all by itself. The problem is that many seekers of Enlightenment are still controlled by the ego mind and want explanations. They do not want to hear that it just happens. They want to run before they can walk. They want detailed step by step instructions of every phase I went through to get to where I am, and even if I could supply them with step by step instructions they would want to jump straight to the last step rather than being patient and letting things happen naturally.

One thing I have learned is that Enlightenment cannot be rushed or forced. The more you have a want or a need for it, the further away it gets. Why does this happen? Because want and need are fear based emotions controlled by the ego mind. The more you feed the ego mind, the stronger it will become. The ego mind will do anything and everything to prevent you from discovering Enlightenment because to become Enlightened would spell the demise of the ego mind. The only way is surrender, and this comes from clearing the mind of uncontrolled thought and dissolving belief systems. So rather than asking how to surrender, follow the example of the first two stages and be patient.

Accepting everyone and everything for what they are without trying to change anything to suit your ideals is an absolutely awesome position to be in. The world suddenly becomes beautiful again. You will observe things in more detail and see more going on around you than you ever did before. Colours become more vibrant. Sounds are clearer. You stop judging people and situations. You have no opinion. Everything is exactly as it should be. Surrender is acceptance and vice versa.

I get asked about whether I experience anger, frustration and jealousy, and most are really surprised when I say yes. Every emotion can be experienced by anyone no matter how Enlightened they are. Emotions are part and parcel of the human condition and there is no real escape from them. The difference is that I now experience emotions in the moment and usually for only a split second. The ego mind allows you to experience these emotions via thoughts of past and future events, things that no longer exist or that may never happen. The experiencing of these emotions creates stress in the mind and body that can lead to illness. Many people hold on to these thoughts for long periods of time, creating more and more stress. Emotions experienced in the moment are part of your body's natural fight or flight responses and are there to help rather than hinder.

If you get to the Surrender stage and you are still experiencing a struggle with your own belief systems and thought processes, then I would suggest going back to part one of the process.

Enlightenment is not a race to be won. There are no prizes for getting there before the next person. Some will find it far easier than others to reach and some may never get there. It all depends on your current mindset and how strong your beliefs, opinions and prejudices are.

Letting go of ego
and surrendering
to all that is,
isn't the end,
it's the beginning
of the real you,
the true self.

Chapter 9

Being

The fourth part of the process is simply 'being'. Enjoying the experience of life without the fear and suffering experienced by most of the world's population. Just to be clear, when I say 'being', I do not mean sitting on top of a mountain in silent meditation for evermore. You can still be 'doing' while you are 'being'. 'Being' simply means to observe the world from a place of inner stillness without judgement or analysis.

Earlier I talked about being the observer of thoughts and feelings to still the mind. In this fourth and final part of the puzzle there is no observer. The mind is still and there is a deep inner peace but there is no one there to observe it. The observer has dissolved leaving no trace behind. I have heard other teachers and Gurus talk about the observer being the true 'I Am', but without the observer being present, who am I? The answer is pure consciousness, the source of all energy and life. This may seem like a strange concept to grasp and some of you may be completely lost by what I am saying, but once you have experienced the previous three stages on this bizarre ride, you will understand this stage without question.

Simply being and viewing your surroundings without judgement while carrying on with your normal daily routine of life and work is a truly awesome position to be in. Nothing will be mundane or boring. You stop watching the clock to see when it is time to go home from work because time is no longer the enemy it once was. Have you ever actually stopped and listened to your friends, family and work colleagues and heard how often they refer to time? How often they state that things will be better at some future time? For example, they may say that they are having an awful day and cannot wait for the day to end, or maybe money is tight and they wish the month away so they can get to payday. If they actually looked at their lives and their state of mind, they would find that time was never actually the problem. When you can allow yourself to simply be and live every moment of your life one second at a time, time becomes irrelevant.

Even though I am in a position of no uncontrolled thought, total acceptance of everything that is and in a state of just being, there is no wow factor attached. I know that those who carry the weight of the world on their shoulders would look at my situation and probably envisage that I walk around in a constant state of euphoria, but as I said in an earlier chapter, if you live in a particular manner for any length of time, whether that be in a good or a bad way, that way of living becomes normal. To a certain extent I would say that some of the wow factor has actually vanished from my previous life. I have always been a positive person and always found something to strive for and to look forward to. That may have been a new business venture, a new car, a holiday, a new job or a new hobby, but now I live very much in the moment away from dreams of the future and also the disappointments of the past. Does this sound like a boring and pointless existence? I'm sure that it does to many people but only from the ego mind's point of view. Without the ego mind there is no boredom.

I am very happy with where I am right now and live an extremely stress free existence. My wife would argue that I am only existing and that my enthusiasm for life has gone. By this, I mean that by simply being I no longer appear to have the get up and go or the enthusiastic approach to life that I used to have. To the outside world looking in, this appears to be a problem or an issue, but only from an ego point of view. My enthusiasm may appear to be lacking on the outside but on the inside I have perfect contentment. I enjoy just being, taking in the sights and sounds of everyday life. Watching the world go by and the interactions between families, friends, enemies, lovers and just about everyone else in between. I have a genuine intrigue and love of watching life and situations unravel before my very eyes.

My story that has led me to where I am today is different from others who have achieved Enlightenment. I didn't have the break downs or the trauma that others had to experience to reach this point, and for that I am grateful. But the one thing I do have in common with these people is that we have all either reached or been through this period of just being. Some experienced it after a break down and had no choice but to be a prisoner in their own home while this period of just being played out. Some had to spend time in far away places in foreign countries, away from the rat race of their normal lives to allow themselves to just be. I was fortunate enough to just be whilst carrying on my normal life and job, although it didn't go unnoticed. The people around me saw a calmer, more relaxed, happier, contented me. Some assumed that there must be a problem for this sudden change in me and that maybe I was putting on a happy front to hide some deeper problems. A few even staged an intervention one night to try to save me from whatever I was hiding from them and wouldn't let me leave until I told them what was going on. How do you tell those close to you what is really going on without them phoning the psychiatric ward and having you committed? For those trapped in the ego mind this stuff is just not normal. I have met others who have experienced a similar state of awareness and decided to 'come out' and tell the world about their Enlightened state. These people tell stories of being ridiculed and alienated by those closest to them and of lost friendships and relationships. Other than my beautiful wife and children, I haven't even told my closest family and friends about any of my experiences. Why would I? It's not a trophy or an achievement to be shouted from the roof tops. It's not something that makes you better than the next person, just different. This book is the first glimpse that my closest family and friends will get into who I really am now, if they read it of course! I'm not the best at explaining things to others and often put my foot in it and say the wrong things. I don't want to alienate anyone, I don't want to upset anyone, and I certainly don't want to make anyone feel inferior in any way. So during my intervention, whilst being backed into a corner and interrogated by my friends, I had to make a choice as to whether to tell them the truth or to lie. The problem was that I didn't really want to do either, so I explained that I had some personal issues that I was dealing with that I didn't want to talk about and that their support was exactly what I needed at that time. I thanked them for 'saving me' and was allowed to leave.

Having just said that Enlightenment is not something to be shouted from the roof tops, it probably hasn't slipped your notice that I have written a book about it and often talk to groups of people about Awareness and living in the moment. I don't think that Enlightenment is something that is owned or is for sale, but I do think that my experiences might just help others who are looking for that inner peace. I see what I have as a gift and it would be selfish not to share it with others. That said, I would never preach it to those who have no interest in it. Those that are interested in making that change will pick up this book and read it or come to a talk to hear what I have to say. Those that are not interested will not be looking for anything and will probably never get to know my name or have any awareness that I have even written a book. Either way works for me.

*Finding time to
do nothing is
the key to
discovering
everything.*

Chapter 10

Happiness

OK, I know what you are thinking; in the last chapter, I said that part four of the process was the final part. I had just about finished writing the book when something new happened to me. It was something that was unexpected and sort of crept up on me, but something that I couldn't leave out of the book, so I had to write another chapter and slot it in. Of course, I could have changed the wording in the previous chapter and then called this chapter the final part of the process but this has made me realise more than ever that maybe this is not the final part of the process. I mentioned earlier in the book that I had no idea if there was more to come or if this state of consciousness would last forever. To be completely honest, I still have no idea. I think that because I had spent so long in the phase of just being, that I had subconsciously accepted that there was no more to come. There may or may not be more phases in the process. Maybe I will write another book! Unlikely, as this one has been two years plus in the making.

So what is this new phase or part in the process that just had to go into this book? Now I don't want you to get too excited, as what I am about to tell you is not some life changing miracle that you would not have been able to live without, but it is something that deserves a place within these pages. I want to be satisfied that I have explained all of my experiences to this point in my life. If anything else changes before I get what I have written so far to the publisher, I may never get this book finished! If you are reading this in book form then I achieved it and actually got it finished. If you are one of my relatives reading this manuscript long after my time on this earth has passed, then I obviously never got it finished. If you would be so kind as to not throw it out with the rest of the dust covered trash that I collected over the years, maybe you might consider getting it published for me!

Enough of the waffling and on to the fifth part of the process, the surprise that has held up the completion of this book. The fifth part in the process is enthusiasm. Yes, enthusiasm. You see although I found an awesome inner peace away from the plague of uncontrolled thoughts of the ego mind and an acceptance of all that is that has allowed me to just be, I did seem to lose the enthusiasm to do anything. Usually, when a person has a lack of enthusiasm it is because of an underlying and sometimes serious condition such as depression or anxiety. My lack of enthusiasm was due to complete and utter contentment in every aspect of my life. I am not even sure that I would call it a lack, as I didn't feel that I was missing anything. Others noticed that I was not displaying the same drive and ambition that I had always had in the past, which is probably the very reason why my close friends thought that I had some serious problems that I needed rescuing from. I was just so happy viewing the world from a place of completeness that I didn't need or want anything. I had no need to strive for greatness or riches. I have no point to prove or arguments to win. I have no desire to be the best at anything. None of this has changed, but I am now in a different place where I am actually enjoying things and enthusiastic about doing certain things.

Whilst in the 'just being' stage I was still going to work and getting things done, and I did it all with a genuine smile on my face because I am very happy with myself. But in the being stage there was no ambition and I seemed to just be going through the motions of getting things done rather than actually getting any enjoyment from them. This does not mean that I was not enjoying what I was doing, in fact there was little or no emotion one way or the other, I was literally just being and doing almost in zombie fashion but with a deep and fulfilling feeling of inner calm. I still have that feeling of inner calm. I still have the same openness and acceptance of all that is. I am still in that just being stage but with a difference. I have regained my past enthusiasm, ambition and enjoyment for life. This may not even seem worthy of a chapter in this book to most of you, but to me it is a massive change because enthusiasm, ambition and drive are usually associated with ego. By this I mean that ambition and drive are generally driven by ego to be better than someone else or to have more than someone else. They are generally driven by greed, jealousy and other negative emotions that keep the ego mind alive. What I am experiencing now is very different. My new found enthusiasm has nothing to do with success, money, power or status but more to do with genuine happiness. Not just happiness for myself but also for anyone and everyone around me. I am doing things that bring me and others happiness without any expectation of financial gain or reciprocation of favours.

I am sure that at some point in everyone's life we will all ask the question 'what is the purpose of our existence on this planet?' No one can truly answer that question but I am fairly certain that our purpose here has nothing to do with suffering. If I had to guess at our purpose in life from my fairly unique point of view, from my place of Awareness, I would have to say that happiness is the key, the reason and sole purpose of our human existence. In this fifth part of my process I have found exactly that, and what's more—I am sharing this happiness with others. If there is one thing that I have learned through my experiences that I would really like to pass on to you it would be that happiness and the effect that your happiness has on others is the most valuable currency there is.

*The meaning of
life is happiness.
The purpose of
life is to share
your happiness
with others.*

Chapter 11

You Cannot Think Enlightenment

Whatever you think Enlightenment is, it is not. I hear people tell me that they get the whole Enlightenment thing intellectually and that although they have not experienced it, they fully understand it. From my own personal experience, whatever you think Enlightenment is, it is not. Enlightenment cannot be thought no matter how many books you read, how many seminars you attend, how many meditation workshops you take part in or how spiritual you think you are. Enlightenment can only be experienced and this is why it is so difficult to explain to others. Words alone cannot describe the depth and feeling of an Enlightened person. I know this sounds like a bit of a cop out and a great way of getting out of explaining what it is but Enlightenment is a Self Awareness that is so simple in its being that all words and explanations are just too complicated to explain it.

I can remember reading books about Enlightenment long before I had even seen a vague glimpse of what it actually was. I lost count of how many times I read 'It just is'. I can also remember my frustration at reading this because I wanted something to analyse and research. To say 'It just is' was ludicrous to me. What just is? What is this 'it' that they constantly drone on about? I wanted a proper, detailed explanation. I now realise that the inner stillness and peace that I experience every moment of every day has no form or space. It has no beginning or end. It is without time or attachment. It cannot be thought. It really just is. Now, how do you explain something like that?

To be able to think something you must be able to picture it in your mind. Enlightenment has no picture because it is not an object. Enlightenment has no sound. It has no feeling or emotion. It has no size or dimension. It cannot be seen, felt, heard or touched; therefore, it cannot be thought, only experienced. Once you have the experience of Enlightenment the explanation of 'It just is' makes so much sense, but only to the person experiencing it. For those not experiencing it this explanation will continue to frustrate, sorry!

A sure fire way not to understand Enlightenment is to try to analyse it. Most seekers of Enlightenment including myself in the early days, research the subject to such depths that they immediately over complicate it and miss the very simplicity of what it is. Don't try to think or understand Enlightenment because you simply cannot do it. You have just read the process that I went through to get to where I am. That process was preceded by me trying to think my way to Enlightenment and by analysing and researching the subject to exhaustion, and it got me absolutely nowhere. I tried to jump straight from ego into Enlightenment by thinking that I had an understanding of what it was all about. By the time I had finally realised that I was on the wrong road to discovering anything of use, I had already wasted months of useless research. I can promise you that the harder you try to reach Enlightenment by thinking you know what it is, the further away you will be from it.

Enlightenment appears to me to be a by product of a set of circumstances that are within your control and thought processes. You need to be able to understand the power and hold that the ego mind has over you before you can find enough clarity of thought to see your own mind for the first time since you were a child. Then and only then will you be able to see the world for what it really is. Gaining an acceptance for things as they are rather than how you used to think they should be. Observing all without prejudice or judgement. Finding inner peace and stillness that will enable you to just be and to tolerate your own silence. Recognising true happiness within yourself without want or need of recognition or reward. Once you have all of these things, something else takes over every fibre of your being, and that thing is Enlightenment, a by-product that you have no control over because it cannot be controlled. This is why it cannot be thought, because it is not a thing or an object that exists separately. It is a collective of many states and circumstances.

Enlightenment is like electricity. You cannot see electricity because it is invisible. Electricity has no smell or taste. It has no colour. The only way to know that electricity is even there is to experience it. Obviously to experience the existence of electricity we can simply switch on an appliance to see if it works. You can also experience electricity by touching it but I am reliably informed that this is a very bad idea so please don't try it at home! When you try to think of electricity as an object you will find it impossible to visualise. Sure you can visualise a spark or an electrical appliance, but these things are not electricity, just by products of electricity. Enlightenment is exactly the same. It is invisible, colourless, tasteless and has no smell. You cannot think it or visualise it, only the by products of it. Just like electricity, Enlightenment is energy. You don't need to think it or visualise it to know it exists; just accept that it is very real and it will find you if and when the circumstances are right.

*There is not a published
word in any book in any
part of the world from
any point in our history
that will help you to
understand Enlightenment.
It can only be experienced,
not thought.*

Chapter 12

Spiritual Qualifications

When you claim to be Enlightened, there will invariably be those who are skeptical and understandably so. Human nature and the ego mind demand proof. I have been bombarded with questions on the subject of Enlightenment, and sadly most of them are aimed at me proving what I say. Many people will be dissatisfied with the answers I give because there is no way of proving or disproving the things I say or claim to be. The great thing is that I have nothing to prove to anyone and have no need or desire to try. Whether people believe me or not, it does not change who or what I am in any way. I will simply carry on as before without any emotional attachment to whether people choose to believe me or not.

One of the most bizarre questions I have been asked is 'what are your spiritual qualifications?'. Out of all of the questions I get asked this is by far my favourite. As if a qualification is all that is needed to be Enlightened. If this were the case, I think everyone would sign up to their local spiritual college and start studying, looking forward to graduation day when everything would become clear upon production of your certificate. Striving toward a qualification to prove your own self worth is just another trick of the ego mind. Is the proof of how clever you are for your benefit or for others? If it is for the benefit of others and you are playing the system to get a job, then there is nothing wrong in that, it's all part of playing the game of life. If it is to prove something to yourself, then this needs to be questioned. If you are not enough in yourself without that qualification, you will never be enough with it.

So what would a spiritual qualification prove? I suppose it could prove that I had read certain books or followed certain teachings that enabled me to answer the examination questions correctly. I'm not sure it could ever prove whether or not I was Enlightened. I know that no matter how hard I tried, I could not write a course or an exam paper that would lead to Enlightenment; unfortunately, it just doesn't work that way. Who would have the right to issue a spiritual qualification? Believe it or not, there are many organisations that do. And once you had your spiritual qualification, what would you do with it? Maybe frame your certificate and hang it on the wall in pride of place where everyone can admire your achievement. Maybe you would use it to show that you are more spiritual than the next person. Maybe you would use it to add value and meaning to your 'spiritual journey'. The problem is that no matter what you used it for, it would be coming from a place of ego rather than a place of inner stillness. The want and need of that qualification, or indeed the want and need of just about anything, is what will keep you from that which you seek.

To answer the original question, which was 'what are your spiritual qualifications?' I would have to say that the answer is none, zero, zilch, nada. Enlightenment is not found in a book (not even this one) or in a classroom. Enlightenment is an experience, and once experienced has no need, want or desire for proof or qualifications.

I suppose that to put things into perspective, if we look at those who we could all probably agree were Enlightened and needed no proof, evidence or qualifications, the two names that stand out are Jesus and Buddha. What qualifications did Jesus or Buddha have? I don't remember a framed certificate hanging on the wall in the picture of the last supper. There is no mention of Buddha having a diploma or degree in Buddhist scriptures. Of course, this does not mean that they were not Enlightened; it just means that they had no need to prove who or what they were. Time has not changed this simple fact. If I had any need or desire to prove anything, then I'm not sure that I could say that I was awake or Enlightened.

My only qualification is my personal experiences, which I am happy to share with the world. Even if I had a formal qualification to show you, I could still only tell you about my personal experiences. My experiences are my qualifications in the same way that your own personal experiences are your qualifications. For what is a qualification if not the learning and knowing of a particular subject? I know about my own life and experiences far more than anyone else on the planet, so I think I can safely say that I am more than qualified to speak about them. But I am only qualified to speak about my own life and experiences because that is all I truly know. I have no idea what others have truly experienced and so I will let them write their own books and tell their own stories.

I have nothing to prove or disprove. When you shine from within, there is no need to step into the spotlight.

Chapter 13

The Spiritual Journey

If indeed we believed that Enlightenment is our natural state that has been masked by social conditioning and belief systems, then we have to also believe that there is no journey because there is no distance to travel to that which is already here. The spiritual journey is something that I hear a lot about. Some people have been on their journey for many years and still appear to be no closer than when they started. If you believe that you need to be on a journey, then you are correct. If you believe that there is no journey, then you are also correct. Confused? Then I'll try to explain. The ego mind is made up of uncontrolled thoughts built on belief systems and social conditioning. Strong, rigid beliefs will keep you in ego and prevent you from locating your inner peace. So by believing that you have to undertake a spiritual journey, the ego will create that journey and keep you there indefinitely. Many people will never complete that journey. If you believe that there is no journey and that Enlightenment is right here, right now, available to everyone and anyone, you are absolutely right. So why is everyone not Enlightened? The answer is the same no matter what you believe, it's the belief itself. Enlightenment comes to those who drop beliefs and surrender to who they really are.

I am sure that if you analyse every word I have used in this book you are sure to find words and phrases such as 'my journey' or 'my path'. I am also sure that my words may have caused some confusion or maybe even have sounded contradictory. Words are obviously not my strong point and it is blatantly obvious that I am not a trained writer. I am, however, trying to use words that somehow make sense to those who have no experience of self-awareness. Phrases such as 'my journey' or 'my path' are used to show the difference between what I used to be and what I am now rather than promoting an actual journey that I set out on. It is clear that I have been through a process to reach this point in my awareness—of that there is no doubt, but that process was more about removing the many layers of beliefs, prejudices and conditionings that had accumulated over the years that had been masking who I really am, who I have always been.

Those who set out on a spiritual journey are more often than not looking for the answers to Enlightenment outside of themselves. That is going to be a very long and lonely journey that will never end unless they discover that the very thing they seek was actually way back at the beginning of that journey within themselves. From my viewpoint the best and simplest way to explain this would be to say that the very thing you are looking for is placed exactly where you are looking from. A lot of you may understand this, but I have a feeling that many more of you will not, hence the reason for writing a book in the first place. Enlightenment is very simple and probably the simplest thing I have ever experienced, but trying to explain that simplicity to an audience of people who look for the most complicated answers to the simplest questions is a challenge, to say the least.

When I look back at my entire life with its many ups and downs, positives and negatives, triumphs and failures, heartaches and heartbreaks, I now realise that none of these things happened to me, they happened around me, and it just so happened that I was there to witness those events and watch them unfold. There were no positives or negatives, just many lessons and experiences that were necessary to become who I am. I could have chosen any path or direction at any point in my life. Every second of every day has been a series of choices leading to various experiences, but no matter what path I chose at any point, they all lead back to the same place, who I really am on the inside. Sure I could have chosen to be a road sweeper or a rocket scientist, two very different professions with very different pay packets and very different lifestyles, but neither profession would change who I really was on the inside. A different choice may bring about a change in attitude or ego, but nothing can change the real person beneath it all.

The next time you think about your spiritual journey, try to picture it in your mind as a road map with many different routes that you could take. You alone have the choice of which direction to go, but this is a road map with a difference. Every road on this map may have many twists and turns but they all lead you back to exactly where you started from. Another way of looking at it is like a maze with no exit. No matter which path you take, you will end up back in the centre, exactly where you started. I'm not sure which path I will take next and what I will experience along the way but I am sure that every path will always lead me back to where I am, where I have always been, and I also believe that I will walk each and every path to experience whatever I need to experience to be me. These paths are not a spiritual journey because I am not looking for a destination on the outside. I know that the destination is on the inside and I never had to go in search of it because it was always here. The paths I choose are to experience the wonders that so many people have right before their eyes but never actually see.

A journey suggests
a distance to travel.
There is no distance
to travel to that
which is already here.

Chapter 14

Sex

OK people, this is getting down to the real grit. I promised to share everything with you, all of my experiences—good and bad. I'm not sure if this subject will be considered good or bad or how well it will be received, and for those of you who are easily offended, have an active imagination or a weak stomach I can only apologise in advance. Just be thankful this is not a picture book! Before you skip past this chapter, I promise that I have not used any foul language, explicit details or tips on sexual positions, although this may actually be disappointing to some of you. I'm just going to keep it real and to the point and hopefully we can get through this section together as quickly as possible without causing too much psychological damage to anyone. This is not Fifty Shades Of Enlightenment.

I am often asked if the experience of having sex is different before and after enlightenment. I don't mind talking about sex and to be honest neither should you. After all it is a normal, healthy activity that should not have any stigma or taboo attached to it. We are all the by product of sex and without it the human race would cease to exist. I appreciate that many people are uncomfortable talking about sex for many different reasons and in a small minority of cases this is justified. For the most part though the discomfort it usually down to two things. Firstly many of us are brought up and taught that talking about sex is a dirty or bad thing. Secondly many people fear sex because of performance issues and body image. The performance fears and body image hang-ups are again products of the ego mind, as are the fear of not satisfying your partner or the fear of rejection.

So is the experience of having sex different after Enlightenment? In my experience it is a definite yes for a couple of different reasons. Firstly, being in the present moment enables one to focus the attention one hundred percent on the act of making love. Secondly, the letting go of the emotional attachment that can cause sexual performance issues are gone so there can be no performance anxiety or fear. For me there was a heightening of all of the senses and the whole sexual experience became more sensual. Without the barrage of the ego's uncontrolled thoughts pouring in, I am able to feel every inch of my body. Not through touch but by just being, feelings flowing from within. I can only pretend to assume that I understand the experience of the female orgasm and multiple orgasms but I now experience waves of pleasure from within that can cause strong muscle contractions around the stomach and pelvic areas. It is a much heightened pleasure that never existed before.

Besides the physical aspects of love making that have changed for me, there is also another aspect that is a little more difficult to explain. The best way to describe it is that both myself and my wife now have much more of an energetic connection than we ever had before. We have always been on the same wavelength as it were and had a healthy physical and mental attraction to each other, but something else has entered our lives, an energetic connection toward one another that really cannot be put into words. We already have love and acceptance, respect and understanding for one another, so that is not it. It is much more of a knowing than it is a feeling. I can't really speak for my wife, although we have discussed this knowing or feeling at length, but for me it is as though she can now see me for who I really am for the very first time. This energetic connection reaches phenomenal heights during love making and as cheesy as it may sound we really do become one on an energetic level.

Another question that has arisen is whether my sex drive or libido has changed. I have read stories which claim that men think about sex as much as every seven seconds. That's 514 times an hour. Or to look at it another way, assuming we are awake for 16 hours a day (and sleep for 8 hours), that's 8228 times a day just while we are awake! That sounds like an awfully big number to me. The Ohio State University carried out their own study by giving almost 300 students hand held clicker counter machines. They divided the students into three groups with each group having an equal amount of male and female test subjects. The first group were asked to record every time they thought about sex, the second group, food, and the third group, sleep. For the purpose of this book we are only looking at the results from the first group. On average the men in the group thought about sex 19 times a day, far lower than the 8228 times a day claimed by other studies. Interestingly though, the women in the group thought about sex an average of 10 times a day. We have no way of knowing if any of these studies are accurate or if the figures change based on age, sex or culture, but they do all agree on two points and that is that men think about sex more often than women and that both men and women do actually think about sex on a regular basis. I can say that I have no uncontrolled thoughts about sex simply because I have no uncontrolled thoughts. I am sure that I have chosen to think about sex from time to time but couldn't even begin to put a number to it. Maybe I need my own clicker counter! As for a change in my sex drive or libido, I don't think there has been. I think I am still pretty much the same as I always was in as much as there are times when I would like to have sex and times that I don't. Like many other men I can rise to the occasion when called upon (no pun intended).

I don't know if other Enlightened people experience sexual pleasure in the same way as me and maybe we are all different and all experience sex in our own way whether Enlightened or not. It's not a conversation that I have had yet and quite a difficult subject to bring up during normal conversation. As I said earlier, I have no issue or embarrassment talking about sex, but I am also keen not to be arrested for talking dirty to people who barely know me.

Now that wasn't so bad was it?

*Life is about who
you are on the inside,
not what you look
like on the outside.*

Chapter 15

Memory

Memory is something one would expect to improve after an awakening, but this was not the case for me. Those close to me actually became quite worried that I was losing my mind and that maybe there was something medically wrong with me. I was called forgetful and often accused of not listening when I could not recall conversations.

I don't know if my experience is different from others, but for me being fully in the present moment means a complete detachment from past and future. When I am asked a question where the answer lies somewhere in the past, I can see the frustration on people's faces when I pause before giving an answer. The answer is just not immediately available to me. It's almost as if I have to reboot my brain or switch into a different mode to find the answer I am looking for. It's as though I have packed the past away in storage boxes in some hidden room in the depths of my mind. The past thoughts and experiences are still there somewhere and may never see the light of day again, but I know roughly where they are if I should ever want to look at them again. The problem comes during conversation when I require information from the past and I have to open all of the boxes to look for the right answer. The worst part is not looking through the boxes, it's trying to remember where the room is where all the boxes are stored! People are not very patient when they are waiting for an answer.

I can't pretend to know why this has happened but if I had to guess or try to give an explanation, I would say that when one is fully in the ego mind the brain is constantly in a state of referring to the past and making up images of the future. In this state the brain is able to very quickly access past information because it is already there. Being in the present moment means that you are further away from those answers. To put it another way, being in the ego mind is like being in a room filled with TV screens, all set to different channels. Each channel is a different event in your life. When you are asked a question about a past event you can look at the screen that is playing that channel. When you are living in the present moment, that room with all of the TV screens and channels still exists, it's just that you are not actually in that room. You are out and about enjoying the experience of life. Now, when you are asked a question about a past event, it takes a little time to walk to the TV room and look for the correct screen. Does that make sense?

So, TV screens, storage boxes, hidden rooms and brain reboots aside, have I managed to explain why I appear to have such a bad memory? Probably not. Other people's frustrations are no real concern of mine because it is exactly that, their frustrations and impatience. I never set out to annoy or frustrate anyone but there is little or nothing I can do to change it. I am in this state of being and extremely happy. I have dealt with my own frustrations over the years and unfortunately everyone has to do the same thing for themselves.

I suppose another way of looking at this is that maybe the things that I am unable to remember are not as important now as they used to be when I was fully in the ego mindset. Some people would have a complete meltdown if someone close to them forgot their Birthday or if a friend momentarily forgot their name. People get stressed every minute of the day over missed appointments and people being late for meetings. Men especially are often accused of not listening to their wives, and to be honest I think that some of them are purposely not listening, sorry guys. But most of them are listening and then genuinely forget what they have heard in an instant. It's all just a part of the human condition that we all have. We all make mistakes, we all forget things. Some forget more than others and at some point we will all have been guilty of forgetting something. There is a very good and scientific reason for this and it has nothing to do with ignorance. The human brain cannot deal with the immense amount of information that it is asked to process every second of every day, so it filters the information by keeping essential info and deleting the non-important, non-life threatening stuff. When you then require some information that your brain has deleted, your brain plays the cruelest trick of all. It fills in the gaps by making stuff up based on past experiences. This is not lying as you will believe every bit of it.

The trouble is others will think you are either lying or were not listening in the first place. This is how the human brain functions in an ego state of mind, so imagine how much more non-essential information it deletes in an Enlightened state. That's my theory, anyway.

The way I look at this memory lapse situation is that if I forget a Birthday or a name, or miss an appointment, so what? No one is going to die. It's not the end of the world. It really is not as important as most people think it is. Maybe its not even that certain things are not important to me but more to do with my not having an emotional attachment to them. There are far more important problems to solve before trying to work out why it is that I cannot remember what I had for dinner yesterday. World hunger, poverty, homelessness, child protection and crime prevention to mention a few. Even these things that we can probably all agree are important issues can be dealt with in much more productive ways when you take away the emotional attachment to them. Please think carefully about this before you shout at me for forgetting another Birthday! Take a look at your daily stresses and the things that people do that really tick you off, then ask yourself how important those issues really are. Is your level of stress going to change a situation that has already passed? Of course not, so take a chill pill and let it go. Remove your emotional attachment from every situation whether they are important or not and see how much more effective you can be in solving those issues.

*I don't have a
poor memory.
I just have nothing
to remember and
nothing to forget.*

Chapter 16

Losing Your Identity

A fear that often arises in those seeking Spiritual Enlightenment is that they will lose their identity and maybe even lose their personality once they become Enlightened. In my experience nothing could be further from the truth. This is one of the many myths surrounding Enlightenment. Enlightenment does not change who you are at your core. It will not suddenly turn you into someone who will be unrecognisable to your friends and family. In fact, for the most part you will remain unchanged on the surface, and many of your previous habits and behaviours will remain unchanged. Enlightenment does not mean that you will suddenly become highly spiritual or religious. It does not mean that you will have to shave your head and start chanting mantras while wearing ceremonial robes, unless you really feel the need to of course.

To ask if Enlightenment will take away your identity is to believe that your ego mind is your identity and that you are your thoughts. The fear of losing your identity is a fear raised by the ego mind. It is the ego mind that is afraid of losing its identity, because Enlightenment is about self-realisation of who you really are, the true 'I Am'. The ego mind's only job is its own survival, and its only weapon is fear. Keeping you in a state of fear is to keep you locked in the ego mind. When you become self-realised or Enlightened the ego mind loses control and the real 'I Am' shines through. But the only thing you will lose is the fear that the ego mind has been controlling you with for most of your life. This fear is not who you were, not your identity.

The question of losing one's identity is a question that I once asked myself. It's a reasonable question until the realisation hits you that the question was being asked by the ego mind rather than by the true 'I Am'. The true 'I Am' would never ask such questions because it has no need or fear. The true 'I Am' has no need for questions or answers, whereas the ego mind can only survive by keeping you in fear by asking questions. If you fear losing your identity you can be assured that you are firmly stuck in the ego mind. If you were not stuck in the ego mind you would not question your identity because you would know the very essence of the true 'I Am'.

I regained my identity when I dropped the ego mind and the questions that it created. The path to self-realisation is littered with questions, doubts and fears all created by the ego. The best way to dissolve the ego mind is not to try to ignore the questions, doubts and fears but to embrace them. That is not to say that you should try to answer the questions raised by the ego mind. You would only be answering the questions from the same ego mind, an internal battle within yourself that is again created by the ego mind to stop you from discovering self-realisation. So how do you deal with the questions, doubts and fears? You simply observe them without analysing them. The further you travel along this path of self-realisation without trying to answer the ego's questions, the fewer questions will be asked. When you run out of questions, you will notice that the doubts and fears are also gone.

The question of losing one's identity is quite amusing to me, looking back on my life. There was a time when I thought that I was losing who I was, and yet I had absolutely no idea who I was. I feared becoming something that those close to me would not like. I put their views and opinions before my own happiness, something that most people do their entire lives. We constantly do things to please other people rather than living the life we choose. Why do we do this? The answer is fear. Fear of not being accepted or not fitting in with other peoples ideals. A fear of rejection. Interestingly though, once you become Enlightened these things have no importance any more. The only acceptance we require is the acceptance of ourselves and all that is. The fear of rejection vanishes into thin air along with all other fears.

I realised a long time ago that whether other people like me, respect me, love me, accept me, reject me or just plain hate me, it makes absolutely no difference to who I really am. Enlightenment brings an inner peace and an acceptance of all things including other people's opinions of you. They are only opinions, not the truth. Even if you tried your very hardest to be liked, loved and respected, you would still find someone who did not like you. You cannot please everyone because everyone has different tastes, so why try to please anyone other than yourself? I'm not saying that you should be selfish or self-centred, just accepting of other people's opinions and likes and dislikes. This way you will be able to discover your true self without fear of what other people may or may not think, and rather than losing your identity you will discover it for the very first time.

A thought has no power until you believe in it. If you believe you are the ego, then that is who you will be.

Chapter 17

Before And After Enlightenment

There is a great saying believed to have come from Buddhist traditions that says 'before Enlightenment fetch wood, carry water. After Enlightenment fetch wood, carry water'. This pretty much means that the person you were before Enlightenment is not that much different from the person you are after Enlightenment. You will still get up in the morning, get dressed, go to work, earn money, eat, sleep, drink, laugh, cry, feel and experience all aspects of this human life. Enlightenment does not mean that you have to lock yourself away from the world and meditate in silence for hours on end. If you are waiting for the miracle that comes from Enlightenment then you will be waiting for a very long time.

Enlightenment is like eating your favourite food. The first time you tasted it you were on cloud nine and it was the greatest thing that you had ever tasted. You then eat it every day and cannot get enough of it, then after a while you realise that it is no longer the amazing tasting food it once was. It still has the same taste and flavour. It is made with the exact same ingredients from the same recipe as before. So why does it no longer have the wow factor that it once had? The answer is its because your taste buds have accepted the taste as normal. In the same way Enlightenment starts out by being this awesome experience with a massive wow factor attached to it, but when you live it and experience it every day it becomes a part of your normal routine. Just as your current lifestyle is a part of your normal routine. Enlightened or not you will continue to work, pay bills, go shopping, eat and sleep just as before.

So, where is the big difference between being Enlightened or not? Why do people spend years on a spiritual journey to get what appears to be exactly what they have now? A great question and one that I get asked whenever I try to explain what Enlightenment is. The answer lies in the fact that most of these people misunderstand what Enlightenment is. It is not a lifestyle change as such because to a large extent your lifestyle will not drastically change. The change is internal and is a massive change. Everything you once thought to be true is shattered and years of belief systems and prejudices disappear. Emotional attachments dissolve. Fear, anger, jealousy and all other negative feelings are gone. For the first time, you are awash with a sense of freedom and calm that can be felt in every cell of your body, a peace and knowing that cannot be explained through words.

One of the unfortunate side effects of life and, in particular, living life trapped inside of the ego mind is that you tend to always look on the outside of yourself for answers. No one really knows the meaning of life or why we are really here on Earth. Maybe its a test, maybe its a punishment or maybe it just is without any reason or meaning whatsoever. People have probably been seeking answers to these questions since the very beginning of the human race. I personally think that the meaning of life is happiness. Of course that does not mean that I am right, it just makes sense to me. I also think that happiness cannot be truly found by looking on the outside. Happiness comes from deep within and has nothing to do with how much money you have, how big your house is, how new your car is, or how many qualifications you have. None of these things will make you happy if you have inner conflict.

I'm not sure that there is an after of Enlightenment because I still do not know how many stages of Enlightenment there are, if indeed there are stages. Maybe this chapter should have been called 'Before and During Enlightenment'. I can vaguely remember who I thought I was before Enlightenment and the turmoil I experienced on the inside. I can remember being stressed and angry over trivial things that held no importance. I can remember them as events but I cannot remember the feelings. The memories are more like images of events that happened to someone else because I have no emotional attachment to them anymore. Most people will have negative experiences throughout their lives and then rather than just having a memory of those experiences, they also carry the emotional attachment around with them like luggage for the rest of their lives. No wonder they feel so over burdened. Each time the memory resurfaces so does the emotion that they felt at the time, even if it is years later. The stress that their body went through at the time of the original event keeps on reoccurring. The removal of this emotional attachment is worth more than all of the riches in the world. The inner calm and contentment is priceless.

It is extremely hard to give you a snap shot of what the before and after of Enlightenment looks like. Trying to explain the value of inner peace and true happiness is a difficult, if not impossible task. The explanation just translates into empty words because they cannot be visualised in the same way as the things that we have been taught will make us happy. The only way to explain inner peace is to demonstrate it. I have wondered that if I took a person out of their normal everyday lives to a faraway place of tranquillity for long enough, would they get a brief glimpse into what inner peace feels like or would the emotional attachment to their old life have too much power? I think maybe this would only work if I took them away from their former lives forever (am I bordering on kidnapping now?). I say this because many people go away on holidays to unwind and escape the stresses of work and family issues. The problem, though, is that in the back of their minds they know that they will soon have to go back to work and back to their families and so they never really relax. You cannot run away from emotional attachments because they come from within and can only be dealt with from within. Enlightenment will set you free from inner turmoil, but If you are seeking Enlightenment to change a lifestyle or to escape your current living conditions, just remember, 'before Enlightenment fetch wood, carry water. After Enlightenment fetch wood, carry water'.

Before Enlightenment
fetch wood, carry water.
After Enlightenment
fetch wood, carry water.

Chapter 18

The Myths of Enlightenment

Whenever I am asked a question about Enlightenment I have no expectation as to the effect the answer will have on the person asking the question. I will always answer in an honest way according to my own personal experiences without fear of causing offence or disappointment. Unfortunately I am not sure that I have achieved this yet as disappointment seems to be the effect of every answer I give. This is largely due to the myths that surround Enlightenment. At this stage of the book I would have shattered most of the illusions you have, but just in case I have missed anything, here is a recap.

Is Enlightenment a long journey?
There is no journey. Enlightenment is who you really are, the very essence of your being. It is internal and cannot be found on the outside. How can you travel to where you already are? Enlightenment is not about going in search of who you really are but the realisation of who you are not.

If I stop all uncontrolled thought, will I be Enlightened?
If only it were that easy (not that stopping uncontrolled thought is easy). I used to think that this was the case until it actually happened. Stopping uncontrolled thought and taking back full control of your mind is only a small step in the process, but in my humble opinion it is a very important step and one that should not be over looked.

Once I become Enlightened, will the ego be gone forever?
The ego mind is never really gone forever because it is a part of you, a part of the human condition. When I talk about dissolving the ego mind I am referring to not allowing yourself to be controlled by it. Ego will pop up every now and then but only in the moment. You will not carry its fears and emotions forward and they will disappear as quickly as they arrived. Try not to look at ego as a negative thing but instead embrace it as a part of you.

After Enlightenment, will all of my problems be gone forever?
A lot depends on what you see as a problem. One person's problems may be another person's challenges. An issue only becomes a problem in your mind and if dealt with from a place of ego the problem is laced with fear. You will have the same issues to deal with after Enlightenment as you did before, you will just view them from a place without fear and other emotional attachments.

After Enlightenment, will I be in a constant state of bliss?
This has not been the case for me. I think this is because after being in a blissful state for a while it becomes normal and just part of the normal routine. I quite often witness other people's behaviour and stop and smile to myself. Those moments are the little reminders of how life used to be for me and how grateful I am to be where I am now.

Is it true that after Enlightenment I will never get ill?
Absolutely not true. How do I know this? Because as I am writing this section I am lying flat on my back after sustaining a back injury! And that is not all. Last month I had one of the most terrible afflictions known to the human race, Man Flu! Unfortunately illness is a side effect of the human condition. This human body is susceptible to allergies, intolerances, breakages, ageing, diseases and all other manner of bacteria and bugs, and there is very little we can do about it. The good news is that Enlightenment brings about a release from the suffering. The ailments will still exist but your experience of them changes.

After Enlightenment, will I live forever?
See the previous question and decide for yourself! There is absolutely no doubt that this human body will deteriorate and fail at some point or another. Death is the one absolute in life, but the energy that is coursing through you is another matter. We know through science that everything and everyone is made up of pure energy, but where does that energy come from when we are born and where does it go to when we die? There is a theory that all energy on this planet has been here since the very beginning and it is just recycled and shared through the various races of people and the

millions of different species of plants and animals. I am not referring to DNA, the Theory of Evolution or even Religion. I am talking about the life force within everything, the essence that allows life. Some might call this the soul and maybe they are right. If the theory is correct then the energy or life force within your body will live on after the body has died. Maybe it will return to Mother Earth, or maybe all or part of it will move into a new body, animal or plant to give new life. Is this the same as reincarnation?

After Enlightenment, will I possess all the knowledge in the universe?

This is a very interesting question and the answer depends on your view on what real knowledge is. If you are looking forward to suddenly possessing the knowledge of rocket scientists and brain surgeons and learning the identity of Jack the Ripper then I'm afraid you will be very disappointed. I have heard tales of people who say they tapped into a higher source of knowledge after an awakening but my understanding of this is that the higher source was in fact self-realisation. When you realise the true self, nothing else will hold as much importance ever again. The old saying 'knowledge is power' holds true, but it is the knowledge of the true self that holds the power and not knowledge gained through qualifications. When one becomes self-realised they hold no power over others but power over themselves and the ego mind.

When I become Enlightened, will I lose my identity?

I can promise that you will not lose your identity because with the ego mind controlling you, you are not who you think you are anyway. Instead of losing your identity, you will actually find it. You will discover who you really are. The question of losing identity is often confused with losing your personality. For the main part your personality comes from the true self and not the ego, so this may not noticeably change. Another point to bear in mind is that the fear of losing your identity is an ego fear. It is a question raised by the ego as a self-defence mechanism. Such fears do not exist without the ego.

Do I have to meditate to become Enlightened?

I have attempted meditation on a few occasions but have to admit that it does very little for me. That said, I cannot deny that many people find a great deal of peace and stillness of the mind through meditation. In my case, stillness of the mind was a stepping stone to Enlightenment but not through meditation in the conventional sense of the word. The technique I used might be considered a vague form of meditation but then so is breathing. Through my experience I don't think that meditation is an absolute must to achieve Enlightenment, but if it works for you then I would suggest continuing with it.

*Do not get caught
up in the need for
Enlightenment, for it
will not make you
any more special.
In fact it will make
you less special,
more ordinary, and
that is beautiful.*

Chapter 19

Falling From Grace

The first part of the process, freeing yourself from uncontrolled thought can lead you into a false sense of security, a false sense of bliss. Being free from uncontrolled thought is an amazing thing and if you have not experienced the sensation that this freedom brings for a long time, if at all, it will feel like a miracle. Indeed it is a miracle, but it is not the full story, only the beginning. Whatever technique works for you to bring about a state of no uncontrolled thought, a break from the ego mind, whether it be meditation, mantras, chanting or prayer, will prove its worth during times of stress, crisis, illness and disaster. A sudden shock can bring about a change in your thinking and take you back to the old habits of the ego mind. I have heard countless stories of those who found peace of mind only to lose it and not be able to get it back. There is the possibility that someone or something will come along and knock you off of your perch. This is not something to be feared as fear itself will keep you locked in the ego mind, but it is something to be aware of and will be a test if it happens.

My big test, the day I fell from Grace, the day I slipped back into the ego mind and a rush of negative thoughts consumed every cell in my body is a day I will never forget. My big test did not come by way of stress, disaster, crisis or illness, it came from stupidity! The greatest gift I had ever been given was snatched away in an instant by Alcohol. I have never been a big drinker and not because I disagree with drinking or even that I dislike drinking, but because the hangovers never get any easier. In fact, they get worse as I get older and the recovery time just gets longer and longer. I attended a friend's summer BBQ where drink seemed to be more of a focus than the food. There were drinking games being played that I kept away from at the start as I knew that I was not a professional drinker. I sat and chatted to several people and had a few drinks along the way, a few more than I should have. Unfortunately my lovely wife thought it would be a great idea to volunteer us both to play one of the drinking games as a husband and wife team, but with one small problem. My wife was driving and so although we were both playing the game, I was now drinking for both of us. The game was quite simple. A table was set up with various alcoholic drinks at either end. A member of each team took it in turns to throw a ping pong ball to the opposite end of the table and try to get it into one of the glasses of booze. If it went in then a member of the other team had to drink whatever was in that glass. Being already under the influence and not seeing straight we lost the first game miserably, and the second game. Apparently the third game ended abruptly when I fell through the table onto the floor and was out for the count. This was at around 4pm. Two of the guests helped my wife to get me home and into bed. I was sick along the way but was blissfully unaware of any of it. That was until I woke up at 4am with the worst headache I have ever had and a mind full of fear. I had no recollection of anything after the second drinking game. I had no idea how I got home. I was terrified and gripped with dread that my inner peace had been replaced with a constant stream of negative thoughts and feelings. No matter what I did, I could not escape my mind. I stayed this way until the following day convinced that I had thrown away such a marvellous gift through nothing more than my own weakness and stupidity. I had taken it all for granted and never even considered the possibility that I could lose it. Thankfully, once the alcohol had left my system and the hangover had subsided enough for me to think straight, I was able to focus on a technique that led me back to mindfulness without too much trouble.

So, do I still drink? Yes, I do but not to excess. I still enjoy a glass of wine when I go out to dinner and maybe a beer or two once in a while, but that's all. I have no fear anymore around alcohol or of losing this precious gift, but it is a lesson that I will not forget in a hurry. It was also a great test and proved that this body was still fragile and could be broken. It showed that I had the strength to triumph over the ego mind and get back to the silence that I had come to love.

Stillness of the mind is a fantastic tool to have and is a life changing phenomena that sadly many people will never get to experience. When I talk of falling from Grace I am referring to the temporary or total loss of this stillness of mind. Enlightenment is something completely different, a much deeper knowing and understanding that is almost impossible to explain. Can Enlightenment be lost? That is a question that I cannot answer. I'm not sure that anyone has the answer to this question, unless of course they have ever lost it. I think that once you realise the true self it would be difficult to lose it, but things happen in this life that can change a person's thinking and diseases that can destroy the mind.

Only the true
self can see
the light in the
darkest places.

Chapter 20

Illness

A great question that often comes up is 'When you are Enlightened can you still become ill?' No matter how many times I try to explain to people that we are still living a human existence in a fragile human body, my answer always seems to prove unsatisfactory. I'm not sure where this myth came from but the assumption that Enlightenment spells the end of all illness has gotten confused with Enlightenment being the end of all suffering, and even that is not the case. Suffering comes in many forms and by far the worst suffering there is has to be the kind we place upon ourselves by way of the negative thoughts we play over and over in our minds that keeps us in a constant state of suffering. That is the job of the ego mind, it's one and only job, to keep us in a state of fear and suffering. It is this very fear and suffering that feeds the ego mind and keeps it alive. This is the suffering that Enlightenment can free us from.

If Enlightenment had the added bonus of never becoming ill, then every Enlightened being that has ever been would still be alive in human form. So now when I am asked this question, I ask that person to think of the most Enlightened person they can think of from any point in our history. Most people usually answer by saying Buddha or Jesus, neither of whom are with us in human form any longer. I've heard a few other answers but the same applies; they all died and left their human form, just as I will, just as you will. It doesn't matter how religious, spiritual or Enlightened you may be this human body will fail at some point. The strange thing is that everyone can accept that Jesus died on a cross and that Buddha died of food poisoning, but they struggle to believe that someone claiming to be Enlightened in this day and age can get ill. We live in a strange and beautiful world.

Try to think of your body as a vehicle, just another mode of transport that allows you to move around. It has some cool attachments such as arms and legs, hands and feet, fingers and toes. It's an awesome vehicle and you are extremely lucky to own it, but every vehicle needs a driver. It doesn't matter how cool your vehicle is if it is driven by a moron! Your vehicle is going to be driven by either the ego or the true self, so which will it be? Assuming that all of you choose the true self to drive your vehicle, there should be no future problems, right? Wrong! If you are into motor sport and watch Formula One racing on TV you will see the best drivers from all around the world in cars built by the best car builders in the world. The cars are maintained by the best mechanics in the world and analysed by some of the most sophisticated computer systems ever built. Millions upon millions of Pounds and Dollars are spent on these cars, drivers, builders, mechanics and computer systems every year, but it still does not prevent that Formula One car from breaking down from time to time. Our bodies are similar to Formula One cars in that they are extremely complex pieces of hardware and extremely fragile. You may be the most Enlightened being ever but the true self is piloting a very sensitive and fragile vehicle through a life littered with dangers. It's just a matter of time before your vehicle or one of its component parts fails and you find yourself in the pit lane looking for a repair or replacement parts.

Illness is not something to be feared but the ego will thrive on fear of illness as well as illness itself. Illness and pain are still experienced once Enlightened but all experience is in the moment rather than the accumulative negative feelings that are the trade mark of the ego. This accumulative effect is the cause of sadness and depression through illness. For example, if you have a bad headache, the longer you have it the more it gets you down. You allow it to weigh you down more and more as time passes even though it is exactly the same headache you had all along, no better, no worse. You feel sorry for yourself and wallow in self-pity, but that is not the true self looking for sympathy, it's the ego. Experiencing pain in the moment is still as painful but without the self pity, negativity, fear, anxiety and depression that usually accompanies it with the ego mind.

Many people including Buddha have said that thoughts become things and what we think we become. If this is true then the fear and depression that accumulates during illness, and I suppose in any life situation, will only bring more fear and depression. In a state of ego mind illness only breaks and subsides once you have accepted it and stopped fearing it, but this goes against the ego's very purpose in life, to keep you in fear. Without fear you can accept illness for what it is without worrying about what it might become. Those trapped inside of the ego mind have one more hurdle to get over even once their illness has passed, and that is dealing with the stored fear and emotion that the illness will return. In this state of mind an illness will quite often return because that is what the ego is telling you and willing you to do. We have all heard friends and family telling us stories of just how ill they were and how frightened they were. They almost enjoy the fear and cannot let it go. They have no idea of the damaging effects caused by carrying around these emotions. If you have no uncontrolled thought, your experience of illness is one of acceptance rather than one of fear. The two experiences are very different but illness is still illness and pain is still pain. This is something that Enlightenment will not change.

*The great storm
of life has no
power when you
learn to dance
in the rain.*

Chapter 21

Death

I have been asked on a number of occasions if I fear death. This is a question that fascinates me, but to answer it openly and honestly it requires some clarification. Is the question 'do you fear death?', or 'do you fear the thought of death?'. These are two very different questions with two very different answers. I am not trying to avoid the question or trying to be clever but this is a serious question that obviously means a lot to those asking it. I want to give as honest an answer as I possibly can and I can only do this if I know exactly what the question is.

If the question is 'do you fear the thought of death?', then the answer would be a straight forward no. The thought of death is a negative thought that I no longer experience. I think if you asked the majority of people if they fear the thought of death they would probably say no because it is quite difficult to contemplate your own demise when it is not imminent. Most people do not contemplate death at all until it is right in front of them. The human race goes about its business as if death did not exist and I guess that just makes life a little simpler to deal with.

If the question is 'do you fear death?', I would have to say that I don't truly know the answer. I don't think I could answer that question until I was about to die. I can't with any certainty say how I will feel when death is upon me. Will I panic? Will I be in a state of fear? Will my ego return with a vengeance? Do any of us truly know how we will feel or react as we are about to pass away? I suppose a lot would depend on the manner of your death, your age and circumstances at that time. There are countless examples of people with terminal illnesses who welcome and embrace death without any fear at all.

Because fear is an element of the ego mind it is difficult to see how someone who has escaped the ego mind can have any fear around death. But the big question is whether we fear death of the person and the body or death of the ego mind? Dissolving the ego mind is a sort of death without dying, or a death before death, if that makes sense. To take away the ego mind is to take away fear. Self discovery, self awareness, consciousness, Enlightenment, call it what you will, this is the start of the end for the ego mind. The biggest fear that the ego mind has ever installed into you is the fear of death of itself. As soon as you start out on the path to self discovery, the meaning of the true self, the battle between the true self and ego will begin. The problem here is that the ego is battle hardened and has been trained in combat and self preservation since the very beginning, whereas the true self is pure and without conflict. The true self has always been there even before the ego existed in your mind, but the ego has become extremely powerful and dominant while the true self has been dormant. It seems like an unfair fight, but the true self has the ultimate weapon against ego, you just have to learn how to use it. So what is this weapon? The weapon is acceptance of all that is without analysis or prejudice. The ego can only survive on fear and when that fear is taken away, it dies quickly. Acceptance removes fear but as soon as you start to analyse a situation or argue a point, fear will creep back in and allow the ego to retake control.

When I talk about the death of the ego, I say it as though the ego were a separate person living inside of you or a dual personality, but the ego is actually a part of you. It never really dies and, in truth, you should not want it to. The ego can be a very useful tool if you control it rather than it controlling you. The true self has been dormant in you for a long time and allowed the ego to take control. It is now time for a shift in power that will allow the true self to rule and the ego to become dormant. Just as the ego thrives on fear the true self thrives on acceptance. Some may tell you that the true self thrives on love but what is love if not total acceptance? True and pure love has no conditions. The shift in power between fear and acceptance can happen very quickly and can be overwhelming, but it is also life changing.

Do we ever really die? If you believe that you are this body then I guess the answer is yes. I have come to realise that I am so much more than this body. I am consciousness, the life force that controls this body. This consciousness has been here forever, and when this body comes to an end the energy that dwells within will survive. It will always be here. It cannot be hurt or destroyed.

It cannot be killed. The energy that flows through this body will go on and flow through other people, other animals and other things forever. Maybe the knowledge and experiences I have had in human form will go with it. As I said earlier, maybe this explains reincarnation and why some people appear to have knowledge and experiences of past lives. This is not something to be feared but something to be embraced and accepted. The death of this human body is not the death of the true self, the life force within you.

I view death very differently than I used to and to some my views may appear cold and uncaring, and yet I am far more compassionate than I ever was before. We mourn the dead and we cry and feel sad. We even revisit that sadness on special occasions such as Birthdays, Christmas and Anniversaries, but are we really mourning the dead or mourning ourselves? Living in the moment takes away the need for sadness and loss and replaces those feelings with gratitude. I am truly grateful for the people who have played a part in my life and although I felt sadness when they passed, it is not a sadness that I can hold on to. Holding on to sadness is just like holding on to any other negative emotion, it will destroy you from the inside out. When I attend funerals I will more often than not cry, but I am not crying for the person lying in the coffin, I am crying for the hurt I see in the living people around me. I get very emotional when I see others suffering. The strange thing is that funerals are not for the dead, they are for the living. Funerals allow loved ones to express their sadness publicly and to show how much they cared, but why do we need to prove our sadness? The true self doesn't need to prove anything, but the ego mind has to keep you in a state of fear and sadness; its very existence depends on it.

*This human
existence is brief.
Make every moment
count, but don't
stop to count
every moment.*

Chapter 22

Non-Duality

Non-duality, everything is one, I am at one with everything and everyone, blah blah blah blah! This is a subject that has been written about countless times. There are seminars and workshops dedicated to non-duality, and unfortunately many people have spent their lives studying the subject without actually finding the inner peace that it promises. For those of you who have absolutely no idea what I am talking about (something I experience a lot of), non-duality or non-dualism is the theory or idea that the entire universe and everything within it that may appear separate are in fact expressions of one essential reality. This is nothing new and a concept that goes back thousands of years through various spiritual traditions and religions.

Science has proved that everyone and everything is made of energy and so everything is connected in that way, but what we see and do in our everyday lives still appears separate because that is the human experience. We know that everything is energy but knowing and seeing and experiencing are completely different things. We view the world through our human eyes, through human filters which have been programmed by our life experiences, social conditioning and belief systems. Everything around us looks and feels separate and that is absolutely fine. The oneness that is often talked about in connection with an Enlightened being from my experience is a knowing rather than an experience. Do not be disappointed that you are not seeing the world as a continuous rainbow of oneness; it's the knowing that will change your view of the world rather than the seeing.

I was once asked if I see the world differently now. My answer was no, I still see exactly what I saw before. I feel the world differently now, I understand the world better than I did, but my eyes still perceive objects and people exactly as they did before. I remember the disappointed look I got when I gave this answer. I know that some people claim that they see auras and colours, and some have claimed to see spirits, angels, fairies and energy. I cannot prove or disprove any of their claims because I cannot see through their eyes, but I don't see any of those things. I have an overwhelming sense of knowing and feeling but when I look at another person, I still see another person. When I look at a chair, it is still a chair. So the theory of non-duality to me is just that, a theory, because I cannot see it or touch it. I cannot prove or disprove it, and the great news is I don't have to. It's not important. It doesn't change who or what anyone or anything is because everything still is. My human experience will not change even if I could prove or disprove non-duality.

I've heard it said that everything we see, hear, touch, smell and feel, is all an illusion, a figment of our own imagination. If this is the case, then everything is one inside of our own imagination. This may be true and it may not be true. I don't know and neither does anyone else. The point I am trying to make is that it doesn't matter. Enlightenment is simple and only as complicated as you want to make it. Trying to prove the illusion or the truth about non-duality will only complicate your journey and clutter your path to Enlightenment. Anything you prove or learn is futile and at some point you will have to let it all go. This doesn't mean that non-duality is either real or unreal; it just means that it is not important in the grand scheme of things. The important thing is the letting go of everything that cannot be proved or disproved, as it is an internal battle that cannot be won.

I will admit that shortly before the early stages of my transition into whatever it is I have now, I did a lot of research into non-duality and got caught up in a web of belief systems surrounding the idea. I became convinced that non-duality was the answer to everything, the answer and key to Enlightenment. Many people have done exactly the same thing and will continue to do so. I soon realised that this was actually a set back in trying to understand Enlightenment, and not because the theory of non-duality is right or wrong but because it cannot be proved or disproved. Anything that cannot be proved or disproved is a waste of your time and effort. Also, trying to find the answers that lead to Enlightenment will actually keep you from it. Enlightenment is not found by soaking up more and more knowledge and trying to understand it. It is found by letting go of all theories and beliefs including non-duality. I know that this will upset a few people but I am also aware that it is not their true self that will be offended because the true self cannot be offended. The ego mind on the other hand will be offended because it will fear its beliefs being challenged. It will fear not being in control of what it has believed to be true for so long.

When you accept
everything for what
it is, there are
no surprises.
Suffering comes
from non-acceptance,
because the ego
mind pictured
things differently.

Chapter 23

Forgiveness

Forgiveness is a delicate subject and one that I will treat very carefully. Most religions rely heavily on forgiveness as a basis for their teachings. On the surface it sounds like an ideal that we should all follow and for many years I believed that forgiveness was the most powerful tool in my arsenal. I can already feel thousands of eyebrows raising as you read this but please stay with me and let me explain why I am about to dismiss forgiveness as the worst tool in anyone's arsenal. Not so many years ago, I probably would have been stoned to death or hung for heresy for even suggesting that forgiveness was a bad thing. But this is not about religion as forgiveness was a concept that existed long before religion did.

From an ego point of view to forgive and forget appears to be what the bigger person would do. Not only does it let the guilty party off of the hook and make them feel better, it also makes you feel better and pumps up your ego. So why is this a problem? Surely to forgive is a win win situation for all involved. The problem is that the ego mind lives in a constant state of judgement and negativity, always looking to find fault with other peoples words and actions. Always looking to defend its own position and prove that it was right, even if it knows that it is wrong. The ego mind acts as a separate entity away from anyone or anything else. The act of forgiveness is nothing more than the ego mind giving itself a pat on the back and letting the other party know that they were in the wrong and you were in the right. If you were totally honest with yourself, when you say that you will forgive and forget, do you ever really forget? If the answer is no then the next question is did you really ever forgive in the first place, or did you just tolerate for the sake of stroking your own ego?

Once you have escaped the ego mind and woken up to consciousness, you will realise the oneness of everyone and everything. You will realise that to forgive is actually to say to someone that they were wrong. To forgive is to see yourself as being separate from everything else. When you feel that sense of oneness you will understand how silly forgiveness really is. Enlightenment dissolves the judgement, prejudice and need to forgive. Everyone appears as a reflection of ourselves and as such there is no one to forgive but ourselves, but in that awareness there is nothing to forgive. I now have a new tool in my arsenal far more powerful than forgiveness and that is acceptance. Acceptance of everything and everyone exactly as they are without a need to change anything. I have heard others talk about a deep love for all things that comes from consciousness, and from my experience I believe that what I call acceptance and what they call love is actually exactly the same thing, just put into different words.

It is important for me to explain that although I am challenging the concept of forgiveness there are still things that annoy and frustrate me in the same way as everyone else. Maybe there is a small difference in the length of time that I let it bother me for but other than that I still live a human existence and still experience human frustrations. I let them go much quicker now than I used to. There was a time when those that caused me frustration would burn in my mind for a long time and I would demand an apology. I now experience frustration in the moment and let it go almost immediately without any ill feeling toward anyone. I accept that the frustration is mine and no matter how annoyed I get, the annoyance and frustration will only hurt me and that no apology will fix that. When others cause us annoyance, most of the time they do so without the intention of annoying us. People make mistakes. We all make mistakes, and yet we get annoyed with others for doing things that we have probably all done at one point or another.

I appreciate that in our society we have laws and rules and punishments for those who purposely set out to hurt others. This is a completely different subject from forgiveness. When we imprison a criminal or apply fines and community service, we do so as not only a punishment but also as a deterrent to them and others to try to prevent further crimes. We do not ask these criminals to beg for forgiveness and the aim is not to give them forgiveness. This subject of this chapter is the forgiveness of petty annoyances and everyday frustrations rather than actual crimes against other people. If you believe in non-duality there can be no crime against others as there are no others. If you believe that we are all one then any crime committed can only be against ourselves or against the single consciousness. But as we see and experience life as being separate we believe in living within the constraints of laws and rules. Would the consciousness that is everything be any different without laws and rules? Society would be different from a human perspective and would go back to survival of the fittest, but consciousness is consciousness and energy is energy, and if everything is one then would that change in our society make any difference at all? Who knows? Who cares? Sorry, please forgive me!

*Enlightenment is not
about seeking perfection.
It is accepting other
people's imperfections.*

Chapter 24

Heart Energy

Follow your heart rather than your head. This is something I have heard, seen and read many times, and I've even preached it myself to others. But if I'm really honest, I never really understood it fully until I woke up to consciousness. It sounded like it was a cool and meaningful thing to say but I never really got it. Once I left the ego mind, my very being started to shift from my head into my body, and in particular into the heart centre. Rather than just thinking, I began to develop a knowing that came from the heart centre. I believe that this knowing comes from the true self, the inner energy and life force of who we really are. Maybe it is this knowing that we call Enlightenment.

To stop any confusion, it would probably be wise to explain that the knowing that I am referring to has absolutely nothing to do with obtaining knowledge. This knowing cannot come from a book or a classroom. There are no schools, colleges or universities that can teach you this knowing. There are no qualifications, diplomas or degrees on the subject. The only teacher on the subject of this kind of knowing already resides within you but has nothing to teach you. Not even Google or Yahoo can help you with this one! I know, it's hard to believe that there is something that Google cannot find. It will find search results and bring up websites that claim to be able to teach you this knowing, but take it from me, they cannot teach you this. They can teach you meditation and relaxation techniques and maybe even mindfulness. Some or all of these things may be the stepping stones needed to lead you to your heart centre and the knowing, but the knowing itself can only be experienced and not taught.

The knowing of the heart centre is a little like the skill of breathing. It's probably one and the same thing actually. Let me explain. Did someone teach you how to breathe? No, of course not. When you were born, maybe the doctor or nurse had to smack your bottom to get you to start breathing. That's how they did it in the old days, maybe they still do, although the baby probably has the right to sue

149

the doctor or nurse now for grievous bodily harm! Oh how times have changed, but only externally. The knowing that is within has always been within you. Without this knowing, you would not be alive and breathing. The same knowing exists in nature all around us. No one taught the trees how to grow leaves or taught bees to make honey. No one taught ducklings how to break out of an egg shell or how to swim for the first time. We are surrounded by these mini miracles everyday and most of us have probably never stopped to notice.

The knowing is not like anything else in our lives. The human race tends to look at doing rather than knowing, external rather than internal. Everyone possesses this knowing and there is no great mystery to unlock it, after all you are still breathing so it must still be there. You never lost your knowing, you just covered it over with layer upon layer of life experiences, beliefs, social conditioning and knowledge. None of these things are necessarily bad and to a certain extent are absolutely necessary as life experiences. Enlightenment is a state of being that we enter this human existence with and gradually lose it through our experiences and conditioning. I think this is just a part of the process of growing up, but Enlightenment is never really lost. The regaining or rediscovery of Enlightenment is a process of unlearning everything you thought to be true and absolute.

Whilst writing this chapter I looked at several search engines on the internet to see what others had to say on the subject. Amazingly there are literally thousands of search results of websites offering to teach Enlightenment and the knowing that is the subject of this chapter. One stood out to me and actually made me smile because the author likened the knowing to driving a car! He explains that when one learns to drive they are full of nerves and fear, but with practice the nerves and fears disappear. The more one drives the more confident they become until they no longer think about changing gears or checking their mirrors, the process is automatic. I don't usually tell anyone they are right or wrong but in my experience, the knowing is nothing like driving a car. The automatic process of getting into a car and driving without thinking is a programmed response. It is something that was taught and stored in the subconscious, and this coupled with muscle memory of carrying out a task such as changing gears and checking mirrors over and over, results in the illusion of driving without thinking. There is an enormous thought process and spacial awareness involved in driving that is totally unlike the knowing of Enlightenment. If they were the same then it would naturally follow that Enlightened beings would be better drivers. The one thing that myself and my wife agree on is that since my awakening I am no longer safe to be on the road!

*You will only see
in the world that
which you carry
in your heart.*

Chapter 25

Religion

I was brought up in a non-religious household. That is not to say that we were atheists, far from it. We never went to church on a Sunday or said Grace at the dinner table before every meal, but we went to weddings, christenings and funerals in churches and joined in with prayers and hymns. My parents never pushed religion, mainly because they were brought up in the same manner, but they also never taught me not to believe. They told me what some people believed and what others did not believe. They gave me the information I needed to make my own choices and I respected them for that. I think that if a person finds happiness and comfort in religion then they should be free to practice it. I also think that if a person does not believe in a God or a religion then he or she should not be attacked for it.

Schools back when I was a kid were not particularly religious, well, not the ones I went to anyway. We said the Lords Prayer during morning assemblies. Once in a while the Vicar from the local church would come into the school and talk to us about the Bible. We had a Religious Education class once a week for an hour, and that was it really. I was not frowned upon for not going to church on Sundays or for not saying prayers before bedtime. Likewise I did not frown upon those who did. I have always had religious and non-religious friends from many different races and religious backgrounds. I have never understood why others cannot do the same. I can only assume that fear and ego play a part in trying to keep races, colours and religions separate. I cannot speak for all that have awakened but I would find it hard to believe that anyone who knows their true self could be so cruel and wicked against others based purely on the colour of their skin or the God that they may or may not pray to.

By the time my own children went to school I had formed some really strong views and opinions on how religion was being taught to our kids. It really used to anger me when my children came home from school and told me what they had learned about Christianity. It angered me because they believed every word of what they were being told, even though the teachings were based on faith rather than fact. My big issue was that they were not telling them about other religions, other beliefs and non-religious views. They were not telling the kids that they had a choice in what they could believe. To my mind, if a parent wanted their child to believe in a particular religion, they had the option to send them to a particular school where they would learn about that religion. At that time, there were no schools that taught children about the various options and religions open to them. Now however, many mainstream schools do just that. I think this is mainly because the world has become a much smaller place and children from various countries, religions and cultures now mix freely in our schools requiring different religious beliefs to be taught.

I still have my own beliefs. I'm not sure whether they can be considered religious or if they are any different from other people's beliefs. By that, I mean that what I believe and what others believe are more than likely the same thing but just described in different words. For example, we have all been taught that God is everywhere, that God created the World and everything in it. We also know that energy is everywhere, that energy is in all things and therefore can be called the creator of all things. So is it reasonable to assume that God and energy are the same thing? Please do not send answers on a postcard. Arguments, battles and wars have been fought over these types of questions. Some may or may not believe in the theory of evolution; after all, it is only a theory. Some may or may not believe in the existence of a God; again this is only faith. No one has been able to prove or disprove these theories and faiths one hundred percent, and yet we still kill each other to try to prove the unprovable. Why? The answer is the ego mind. Once you leave the ego mind behind, these questions and battles will be left behind with it.

So, how has Enlightenment changed my view of God and religion? To be honest, my view hasn't really changed at all. I still think that people should have the freedom to believe in whatever they want whether that be religion, Enlightenment or the existence of aliens.

Maybe one thing that has changed is my perception of what God is. I used to think of God as a person or a being and most probably because I had been told at school that we were all created in God's image. I took that to mean that we looked like God and that God had arms and legs and a body and head just as we do. I was also taught that God is everywhere and everything. I was always confused by this as we could not see God. How can we not see him if he is everywhere? I apologise for using words such as he and him, I am in no way assuming that God is either male or female! I have asked friends of various religions where God is and of course the standard answer is Heaven. I then asked where is heaven? Most people automatically look upwards, but we have been upwards, we have been through the clouds and into space. We have telescopes that can see further than we could travel in ten lifetimes, but we still cannot see this place called Heaven. I now think that this is Heaven, right here on Earth. I also think that God is the energy that is everywhere and everything. God is the life force inside of us all. We were created in God's image because we are God. I may use different words to those who consider themselves religious, but I think that science and religion share an awful lot more than either side would care to admit.

*To follow a religion
is to live by someone
else's experiences.
Enlightenment is to
have your own experiences.*

Chapter 26

Explaining The Unexplainable

I have been asked many times to explain Enlightenment. What is it? It's actually far easier to explain what it is not, which is covered elsewhere in the book. Enlightenment is the simplest thing ever and yet the most difficult and complicated thing to explain. It has no words or descriptions that actually do it justice because it just is. It cannot be thought on an intellectual level. It cannot be felt because it has no emotions, it has no fear or prejudice. It has no love or hate. It has no beginning and it has no end. It is simplicity itself. Even the simplest words are too complicated to explain it. It's a something and a nothing all at the same time. I am sure that there are many people who would read this explanation and wonder why on earth they would want something that is nothing because we have been taught to want more, not less. Enlightenment is not something to be gained because you already have it; it's all of the other baggage that you carry around in your mind that must be lost before you can realise what you always had.

Imagine if you could remove all of your uncontrolled thoughts of past and future, your beliefs and opinions, your emotional attachments, your social conditioning and anything you have ever learned. Now replace all of this with the ability to live every second of your life in the present moment. Add to this an acceptance of everything just the way it is without judgement or analysis. Accept all possibilities including religious, spiritual and scientific arguments. With all of these changes comes recognition of an inner stillness, a subtle knowing. At the centre of this stillness and knowing resides the true you. This inner stillness is often referred to as a space, but there is no space, no size or volume. Now, tell me how you explain that! My explanation will form thoughts in your mind of what you understand Enlightenment to be, but Enlightenment cannot be thought. Whatever you think it is it is not. My explanations may even form pictures in your mind of what you think Enlightenment looks like, but it doesn't look like anything.

Trying to explain Enlightenment to those who have not experienced it is like explaining a colour to a blind man. Many years ago I worked in Thailand for a utility company. My job was to train Thai workers how to find and fix leaks in water pipes. You can probably imagine the difficulty in teaching through an interpreter, well, two interpreters actually as we had one Thai national translating English to Thai and one English national translating Thai to English. It was thought that by having two translators of both nationalities we could speed up the teaching. That was the theory, anyway. Unfortunately in practice it just complicated things further. Add to this the fact that a lot of our English words have no translation in Thai. It was difficult and frustrating for myself and my students and was a slow and painful process. But that was not the worst part of it. The Thai workers that I was attempting to teach lived in villages miles from any of the big cities. Most of them had never even seen a tap before let alone a water main. Trying to explain what a water treatment plant was and how water was delivered to thousands of homes and businesses in and around Bangkok seemed like an impossible dream to these guys. Until recently, I thought that this had been the most difficult thing I had ever had to explain to anyone. I was wrong! At least I could take the Thai workers to a water treatment plant and show them a tap with running water. I could also show them diagrams and photographs. I cannot take anyone to Enlightenment or show diagrams. You cannot photograph Enlightenment.

The explanation of Enlightenment always sounds like an avoidance of the question because it appears so vague. The truth is, there is nothing to avoid because there is nothing to explain. The strangest part of this is that those who discover Enlightenment want to share it with the world. They want to help others to find their own inner peace. They want to give the gift to everyone, but we learn very quickly that it is not something that can be given. It cannot be found for you by someone else. Only you can find your own inner peace and stillness. People like myself can light the way. I can show you the door but I cannot walk through it for you, only you can do that. The steps in the process as explained earlier in the book are not Enlightenment, but these are the steps that I took that lead me to where I am right now.

Let me try this. Take a piece of paper and draw a little stick man or woman in the centre of the page. Now draw a circle around it and then another circle around the previous circle. Continue drawing circles until you have seven circles surrounding your stick person. You are the stick person and the outermost circle is the ego mind. Trapped within the boundary of the ego mind are the other circles which are labelled Beliefs, Social Conditioning, Fear, Emotional Attachment, Personal Experiences and Thoughts of Past and Future (which is the innermost circle). Outside of the outermost circle lies infinite possibilities without boundaries including Acceptance, Surrender, Serenity, Peace and Stillness all just waiting for the true self to break through the circles to reach them. When the true self breaks free and meets with the infinite possibilities beyond the ego mind, Enlightenment awaits. You could try to remove each layer or circle one at a time until you had no circles left, but with just the removal of the innermost circle the other circles would dissolve. Without thoughts of past and future the ego mind cannot survive and the other circles would quickly disappear. Similarly if you could remove the outer circle none of the other circles can survive, but the outer circle is strong and extremely difficult to remove. The biggest mistake made by seekers of the true self is that they try to remove all of the inner circles other than the innermost circle in the belief that it will free them. They do not realise how powerful the ego mind is. It will let them toy with the inner circles and play tricks to make you believe that you are making progress. You may even think that some of the circles are gone until a particular event or situation arises and you realise that you are back to square one (sorry, circle one!). All the time that the outer circle exists you will be trapped inside of the ego mind. The ego mind is far too powerful to attack head on but its Achilles heel is the innermost circle, Thoughts of Past and Future. It is important to realise that these circles only exist in your mind. They are not physical barriers but mental barriers. Physical barriers would be far easier to remove.

What remains when
nothing remains?
Even nothing
is something.

Chapter 27

Our Wonderful World

How often do we hear someone say that we live in a wicked and cruel world? How often have you said it yourself? Every time we switch on the TV or read a newspaper we are confronted with all of the doom and gloom this planet has to offer. From a very young age we are subjected to negativity that trains our minds to believe that the world is a dark, evil place. We are conditioned to only see the bad in this world. But once we learn to step out of ego and away from the limiting fears and beliefs that have been ingrained in us, we can begin to realise and to see that this really is a beautiful planet and that the good far outweighs the bad. There is no denying that in some parts of the world life can be very harsh through poverty, war, drought and tyranny, but this is a very small percentage of the world.

Another negativity that has gripped the planet in recent years is the belief that the human race is destroying the planet. Global warming, pollution, hunting, fishing and deforestation are all things that are causing concern. I have no doubt that our actions are having an impact on wildlife, weather and pollution and that a change in our living habits is necessary to sustain a decent level of existence for future generations, but when you look at the bigger picture you will see a different perspective. This planet was here for millions of years before we arrived and it will no doubt be here for millions of years after we are gone. Mother Nature is far more powerful than we give her credit for and she will bounce back bigger and stronger than ever. It's also worth remembering that the freak weather patterns we have experienced in recent years have all happened before. This planet has seen tsunamis, floods, hurricanes, earthquakes and volcanic eruptions before we arrived on the planet, but the planet survived. We simply cannot destroy the planet, we can only change it.

So what about the extinction of animals? It is blatantly obvious that the human race is having a massive impact on wildlife and that certain species have gone out of existence because of us. It is also true that millions of species have become extinct without our help.

The human race will no doubt itself become extinct and something will take our place as the dominant species. So is the coming and going of species just the natural order of things? Is it supposed to be this way? Earlier in the book I talked about death and how we are made of energy, as is every animal, plant and tree on the planet. Through science we know that energy never really dies, it just returns back to source. Therefore animals never really die. Their bodies may come to an end, but their soul or consciousness remains. This gets passed on to the next species and then the next.

We have all heard it said that money is the root of all evil, usually said by people who have no money! The evil of money is only ever talked about when it is in large sums. Most of us use money in one way or another everyday of the week and never consider our purchases to be evil in any way. Money is just another energy and holds no evil. The evil comes from fear of loss from those who have money, and jealousy from those who do not. Both fear and jealousy are products of ego. The evil comes from within the minds of people and not from paper money and coins. Money has been responsible for buying the materials to build the home in which you live. It has fed you and clothed you. It has educated you. It has paid for the doctors, nurses and hospitals that you have relied on to keep you healthy. It has bought expensive machinery that has saved lives. It has paid for medical research that has prolonged life. It has paid for the many inventions that have become a part of our everyday lives. Money has been at the root of everything that we take for granted, so how can it be the root of all evil? There is another saying, money can't buy you happiness. I think that money can buy the illusion of happiness, a temporary respite from unhappiness, but true happiness cannot be bought.

The positives of this world are all around us all of the time. The planet is a beautiful place if you are able to see through the ugliness. Unfortunately many people have been conditioned to see only ugliness, evil and the bad things in the world. Many people thrive on the misery of others. Why else would they subject themselves to watching the news on TV or reading the daily newspapers? I'm not suggesting that we should pretend that bad things never happen or that we bury our heads in the san d and hope that it all goes away. My point here is that watching negativity on the news on TV or reading about it in the newspapers does not change what has happened. Those events have already passed and cannot be changed. The only thing that will change is your perception of the world, your beliefs and opinions and ultimately your own mood. Negativity can only add more negativity. Switch off the TV, put down the newspaper, step outside and take a good look around. Make it your mission to only pick out the positives that you can see, hear and feel. Be grateful for the good things rather than bitter about the bad things. If you do this for just a couple of days you will begin to feel a difference within yourself and start to realise that this really is a wonderful world.

*If you concentrate on
what lies behind you
or what lies in front
of you, you will miss
the happiness that
lies inside of you.*

Chapter 28

Sleep

One of the more surprising side effects of my awakening has been the change in my sleep pattern. I have always loved my sleep and have enjoyed my eight hours a night as a minimum. I used to really enjoy a lie in wherever possible and could stay tucked up in bed until lunchtime. Even if I went to bed at 10pm, I could still sleep right through to the following lunchtime. Now fast forward to my present situation and I am finding that as little as three hours sleep is more than enough to recharge my batteries. I tend to stay up much later than before and rarely go to bed before midnight. At around 3am I wake up as bright as a button. I can only liken it to having jet lag, the hell of all travellers' ailments. If you have ever suffered jet lag you will know what I mean. Jet lag sufferers wake up at some ridiculous hour, bright eyed and bushy tailed, full of energy. They try to trick their brain into thinking they can go back to sleep but the brain is having none of it. The brain is wide awake and fully in control of the situation. It is like a sergeant major at an early morning roll call, barking orders at every cell in your body to be alert. You are completely powerless to do anything other than obey and be awake. The next problem comes halfway through the daytime when you should be awake but can't keep your eyes open. Fortunately my situation does not include this part.

You would think that trying to survive on only 3 or 4 hours sleep each night, one would eventually run out of energy and finally crash and burn. This doesn't seem to have been the case for me. My body seems quite happy with the minimal sleep pattern and actually seems to thrive on it. I'm not getting to lunchtime and then suddenly running out of steam. If I sit down on the sofa during the afternoon I am still known to nod off for half an hour, but not because I feel tired. With or without the afternoon power nap, I am still able to stay up till midnight or later without feeling shattered. I am not sure if this is a permanent condition but it appears to have been this way for quite some time now. Maybe it will change, maybe not.

My personal view on this new sleep pattern is that the ego mind is in a constant state of uncontrolled thought flowing in. Uncontrolled thought is always negative and with it comes stress. Stress releases a stream of hormones into the body that then has to be pumped around the body by the heart and absorbed by various organs. All of this takes a great deal of energy. The knock on effect of this is that the body will need more sleep to compensate for the extra workload. Of course, if the mind has no uncontrolled thought to deal with, no stress hormones are released into the body and thus the body has far less work to do. Without uncontrolled thought and stress, the body uses less energy and needs less sleep. Well, at least that is my theory based on my experience. I am sure that more scientific thinkers have a better explanation based on actual research and facts, but my theory just seems to make sense to me.

The strange thing is that while I am awake in the early hours of the morning, I have no uncontrolled thought, no stress, no frustration, no boredom and no loneliness. I am just being in my own silence. That doesn't mean necessarily that I sit still in silence for hours on end, although that is sometimes the case. Sometimes I read, sometimes I write and sometimes I surf the internet. No matter what I am doing, I am happy doing it and happy just being. I have found that the best time to get any work done is in the early hours of the morning when everyone else is fast asleep. There are no distractions at all at that time of day. No telephones, no one sending me text messages or emails. Just silence and space to get things done. When you are trapped inside the ego mind you tend to crave silence and will often look for an escape by way of being alone somewhere. The problem here is that the silence you crave is not really from outside distractions but from the noise created by your own mind. You cannot escape such noise by hiding away because the noise will follow wherever you go. I think I used to sleep deeper and longer when I was in ego because my sleep time was the only time that my mind was still and silent.

Strangely, there are some nights when I sleep for much longer. This does not happen very often and there does not appear to be a pattern to it. There have even been rare evenings when I am getting heavy eyes by about 9pm. Again, this happens very rarely. Maybe every now and then, my body needs a bit of extra sleep to make up for the many nights when I have only had two or three hours' sleep. It make no difference though whether I have had one or ten hours sleep, I wake up feeling exactly the same way, refreshed and ready to start the day. I have always been a morning person and whether I have slept or not, I still spring out of bed in the mornings. I have often wondered if those of you who are not morning people wake up feeling shattered because of uncontrolled thoughts about the day ahead of you. If you are not happy with your job, school, college, university or some other situation that you are not looking forward to, maybe the playing over of various scenarios that may or may not happen are just too much for your brain to cope with. Your stress levels will be raised and the body will require more energy to deal with the thought processes. This is just another of my theories and not based on anything factual. Maybe we should all sleep on it!

*The most surprising
thing about my
awakening was seeing
that everyone else
was still asleep.*

Chapter 29

Communication

Communicating with others on a daily basis is something that has never come as a problem to me. I have been known to be shy, but it has never stopped me from being able to talk to people. Some have said that I could talk for England. I have always been able to talk for hours on end about absolutely nothing. Many years ago, there was a popular TV programme called 'Kung Fu' starring David Carradine, a show I followed religiously. A spin off from the show was a set of collectible trump cards that had kids in a collecting frenzy. I was no different and made it my mission to collect them all. On the backs of the cards were quotes entitled 'Wisdom of the Kung Fu'. One of those quotes that has always stuck in my mind was 'The man that speaks at great length says very little'. That man was me! I could talk and talk without actually saying anything at all, nothing of use anyway. Now, don't get me wrong, I can still talk for England and still have long conversations about nothing much at all, but I'm now fully aware of it, both in myself and in others. This part of communicating is still a lot of fun. The bit that has changed in me is communicating with people that are so trapped in their ego mind that they cannot see the wood for the trees.

When two ego minds communicate, they feed each other constantly with fear, doubt and negativity without realising they are doing it. Many of those conversations will include disagreements, arguments, resentments, jealousy, guilt and defending emotional positions that the person probably doesn't even believe themselves. That is human nature at its worst when trapped in the ego mind. When communication occurs between two self-realised people, the conversation is very different. There is no need to prove a point or to prove who is right or wrong. There is no emotional position to defend and therefore no arguments or disagreements, no resentment and no jealousy. This is all well and good if a conversation actually happens between two self-realised people. More and more people are becoming Enlightened every day and much faster than they ever did before, but meeting them on a regular basis is something that I have still not achieved. These people are still very few and far between and so I find myself communicating on a daily basis with those trapped in the ego mind.

The only way to communicate with a person trapped in ego is to treat every conversation as a game. The reason being that you do not want to feed their ego by agreeing with something you believe to be wrong or by disagreeing and drawing their ego into an argument, and of course, you cannot just sit in silence as they will assume that there is something wrong. It's a very difficult game to play and one that is very finely balanced. It's a game that takes practice and one that I still have not mastered, but I keep on trying as the only other option is to never speak to anyone ever again. This is not really an option in our little corner of the world as it would mean not communicating with those closest to us including friends and family. Playing the game has become a massive part of my life and is becoming more and more fun. To some it may sound really false to pretend to be someone you are not and you would be absolutely right. There was a time when I would have shared your viewpoint but I ask you not to judge unless you have experienced what it is like to tell someone trapped in ego that you are a self-realised individual. Believe me when I say that it never goes down in conversation very well.

Enlightenment is not something I ever bring up in conversation unless I am asked and usually only in the company of those seeking their own answers. I do not shout it from the rooftops because it is not something to brag about or shout about. Why write a book about my experiences, then? A great question that deserves an equally great answer, unfortunately I do not have a great answer, just a very simple one. I still believe that I have been given a gift and that my experiences should be shared with others who may need help understanding. My experiences might just help someone to find their own true self. I have tried a couple of meeting group scenarios that didn't really go to plan even though I had no expectations. Maybe I thought that by creating a meeting group, I would attract like-minded people looking for help. Some of the people who came along were just that, but the majority were there to attack and disagree and to tell me I was wrong. How on earth can you tell someone that their own personal experiences are wrong? The meeting groups did not attract those who really wanted to know what Enlightenment was like or those who would benefit from my experiences and so I decided to try another avenue by putting my experiences into a book. I don't know if this avenue will lay me open to the same level of attack or if I will succeed in helping others. Either way, it will not change who I am or what has happened to me. I have been asked if I am worried about close family and friends reading this book, those who have no idea of who I really am. My answer is an absolute no for three very good reasons. Firstly, I do not worry about anything anymore. Secondly, unless you are looking for answers about self discovery and Enlightenment, you would never even know that this book existed and my close family and friends have not yet reached a point in their lives where they are seeking those answers. And thirdly, because they have no idea what Enlightenment is! If they happen to discover this book and ask me why I never told them or if they ridicule me as others have, then I will deal with that as I do everything else—in the moment.

When I do manage to get into a conversation with someone who is genuinely interested in my experiences, I become intrigued by their experiences. It never ceases to amaze me how differently we all experience things, how two people can witness exactly the same event and yet recall it so differently. Those conversations are extremely rare and so I continue to play the game. I pretend to be as much in ego as the person I am speaking to.

There is a reason
for the people
who enter our lives.
Talk to them.
Learn from them.
Be grateful for them.

Chapter 30

Love

Many publications regarding Enlightenment, spirituality, religion and meditation, talk about love as the ultimate goal in life. This type of love is not quite the same as the affection we express for our friends and family or the bond that we have with our children. This is more of a universal love for everything in existence. On the surface, it appears to be quite a hippy, flower power view of the world. I used to think that the suggestion was for us to view the horrors that happen around the world everyday through rose tinted glasses and pretend that it isn't really happening. I never really understood how someone could love everyone and everything when so much of it was so bad. It felt really false to pretend that everything was fantastic when it so obviously wasn't. I understand it all a little bit better now but I have questioned myself about what love really is and what it means to me. Love may mean something completely different to you and only you will ever know what that is.

So what is love? I have just mentioned the feelings we have for family and friends and the bond we have with our children, but is this love or is it something else? Is it more of a familiarity than love? Is it human nature to look out for and protect our nearest and dearest? Is it a duty instilled in us? When we 'fall in love' many people experience butterflies and all manner of emotional side effects, but is this love or just a series of chemical reactions? Lots of questions that have no real answers. The dictionary has several definitions for love, here are just a few:

- To like another adult very much and be romantically and sexually attracted to them.

- To have strong feelings of liking for a friend or person in your family.

- To like something very much.

All of the above definitions mention a strong liking for someone or something, but is love much more than just a liking? When I hear people talk about either liking or loving someone or something, there is a very big difference between the two. I don't even think that a very strong liking explains love. Love appears to be so much more than just liking, and again I suppose that those feelings are unique to each individual.

To me, love is acceptance and in certain circumstances tolerance. For example, we will tolerate certain behaviour from our own children that we would never tolerate from other people because we accept our children for who and what they are. We tolerate the behaviour and habits of family and friends because we accept their flaws. Married couples may have pet hates and dislikes for one another but they stay married because they tolerate those pet hates and whole heartedly accept them. Sometimes it is the flaws in a person that creates their unique character and makes them attractive to others. Enlightenment doesn't really change this and I know that I have many flaws that annoy the hell out of my wife on a daily basis, but she tolerates them. Likewise, she has certain behaviours and habits that make her unique. I can't say that they annoy me anymore so I suppose that has changed, but there are still moments when I disagree with something she may have said or done. The strange thing is, I wouldn't change her even if I could. My total acceptance of who and what my wife is, coupled with that deep sense of knowing that happens when she walks into a room and the emptiness I experience when she is not around, that's love.

From my experience, universal love is actually universal acceptance of everything exactly as it is without trying or wanting to change it. On the surface, this may look like the same type of love that I have just explained for people, but universal love or acceptance takes a great deal more inner strength that can only be found through self-discovery. For example, when we see or hear about a murder, our first reaction is usually one of sadness for that person, but that person has no sadness because they have passed. Our next reaction is usually anger and revenge, but no amount of anger or hatred will change what is already done. These feelings and emotions will

186

release stress hormones into your blood stream, which, if allowed to build up over long periods of time, will cause you illness, and in extreme cases, death. I am not suggesting that you should not care about murder or any other atrocity. I'm not suggesting that the murderer should not be caught and put behind bars. I am suggesting that you accept the fact that you cannot change what has happened and therefore there is absolutely no point in putting stress on your body. Your morals and sense of right and wrong do not change but the emotional attachment is removed. I don't accept that bad things should happen but I totally accept that bad things can and will happen. Acceptance of all possibilities good and bad. Acceptance of what is rather than what should be.

Whether you want to call it love, acceptance or tolerance, I don't think that it is the ultimate goal in life. Everyone has different goals and ambitions, whether it be money, career, relationships, property, vehicles, holidays or hobbies, but all of these things aim at the same end result, happiness. The pursuit of happiness is where most people put their energy, striving for that feel good factor. The problem is that none of these things last for very long and before you know it you are out looking for more. But true and lasting happiness can be found through total acceptance. Total acceptance is found by surrendering to all possibilities without judgement. In this way love can be explained as acceptance of all things without judgement, criticism or prejudice. This is not to say that I do not find fault with things in the moment or have the occasional moan, but in the grand scheme of things I have found a deep acceptance and infinite possibilities in everything. I think this is a huge part of Enlightenment. This is not something that I suddenly woke up with one day, it was a gradual process that grew with time. Just like the whole concept of Enlightenment, total acceptance is a deep and filling inner knowing of all that is. It is very difficult to explain with words and would need to be experienced rather than explained.

How long
you live is
not important.
How deeply
you love is.

Chapter 31

Life

On the inside, life is massively different for me now and yet on the surface I'm still the same as I always was. My wife and children have seen an extreme change in me and I think that only those who are around me day in and day out would notice a difference. I have learned to 'Play The Game' when I am around other people and have found that this game of pretend is necessary to get by in the real world. Many people are simply not ready to either understand or accept that there is another way to experience this short life. Maybe they will understand one day, maybe not. If you had met me a few years ago, you would have said that I was the most unlikely person to get to where I am now, that I would never understand or even try to understand. There are some people that I think will never allow themselves to understand, but I know from my own experience that anything is possible and anyone can have a sudden change. In my case there was no life changing disaster or breakdown although I know this has been the catalyst for many that have awakened. We never know when a shift in our lives is going to make sudden and drastic changes for the better or worse, so even with the most unlikely candidates for Enlightenment, I never say never.

I used to view my past as a minefield of mistakes and disasters but, being a fairly positive person, I tried to convince myself that these were learning experiences to help me grow and move forward. My biggest problem was that I was constantly looking to the past and future for the answers rather than living in the moment. I was missing the life that was right in front of me. I have now realised that every mistake and disaster has led me to where I am. Without those events, I would never have reached this point and for that I am grateful. I don't know if our story is already written or if we really have choices, but my life looks as though someone carefully planned every step I took, every experience—good or bad—to make sure I arrived here. If I look back now at that minefield it has been tidied up and looks like a perfectly straight line. It doesn't look or feel like the disaster I once thought it was and I have absolutely no regrets.

The future is made up of lots and lots of nows and everything you do right now is shaping your future. It's a bit like a slideshow and every slide is a moment in time, a now moment. The quality of the whole slideshow can only be as good as the individual slides you have created. We have all seen the neighbour's dreaded holiday slideshows. Some are really fall asleep boring and others are full of exciting 'wish you were here' moments. Ok, there will always be the odd slide that is a bit awkward and shouldn't be in there with the rest of them, but that's life. Planning for the future is not necessarily a bad thing, but it is a pointless task if your now moments do not follow the plan. If all of your now moments are stress free then your future is shaping up to be stress free too, but if you plan a stress free future and then live your now moments in a stressful state, you are planning to fail. Take a good look at the moments you are creating right now. Do they match your future plans? If they do not match then don't worry about it, that moment has already passed. Make the next moment match your plan, and the next, and the next. Before you know it you will have a slideshow full of the right moments. You may make mistakes along the way and that is ok, that's all just a part of the human experience. It's how you handle those mistakes and deal with the consequences that count. A mistake is just another now moment but is only one moment.

The Enlightened person is not that much different on the surface. For the majority of the time their lives follow the same patterns as anyone else and still include working, paying the bills, shopping for groceries, taking holidays and walking the dog. In terms of money they are no richer or poorer than their neighbours. They still plan for the future and learn from the past but they do not live their lives in the past or future. They do not stress about past or future events. They use the past and future as tools that can be very useful when they are not controlled by them. You could be living next door to an Enlightened person and never know it. One of your work colleagues may have had an awakening that no one has noticed. We are just the same as everyone else with one small difference; we live life rather than suffer life. Every experience whether good or bad is just another experience. It may still feel good or bad in the moment, but in the next moment the emotional attachment is gone and the event becomes another experience, just another lesson or learning curve. Enlightenment is nothing to brag about or to shout from the rooftops. It doesn't make me special or superior to anyone else. It also doesn't make me inferior to anyone else, but I have accepted that people react in a negative way to the things that they do not understand. They tend to have strong opinions rather than trying to understand. I also accept that this may not be their true nature and they may be under the influence of the ego mind. I have been questioned, ridiculed, criticised and laughed at for my view of the world and my explanation of my experiences. Many people would have reacted in a negative manner had they come under the same attack, but to me, it is all just another experience. I am grateful to be different and to be free to live my life. People may laugh at me because I am different. I smile because they are all the same.

*No matter how good
or bad your life
may appear to be,
everyday be grateful
that you have a life.*

Chapter 32

The Keys To Consciousness

1.   Observe your thoughts.
2.   Question your beliefs and opinions.
3.   Surrender to all that is.
4.   Just be.
5.   Be happy.

So, having explained the process I went through and the various things that I have experienced along the way, I'll summarise the steps that may help you to achieve a similar or maybe even the same level of Awareness. I would suggest reading this book fully twice to make sure you have not missed or forgotten anything and then continue referring back to this chapter as a constant reminder of the steps, or 'Keys To Consciousness' as shown above. Make it your daily ritual to visit this chapter. Use it as a checklist to make sure you are covering all of the steps. Write the steps on a Post-it note, or several Post-it notes and stick them to your desk, computer screen, kettle, microwave, tv, car dash board and anywhere else that will give you a constant reminder and prevent you from being consumed by the ego mind.

It really can be as simple as you want to make it. The human race seems to want to over complicate everything, its just a part of our programming. But it doesn't have to be this way, I am living proof of that. The five simple steps above are all there is to it and three of those steps you have no real control over. If you can conquer steps one and two then steps three, four and five will naturally just fall into place. So lets have a recap.

Observe your thoughts

Remember that we are only observing our thoughts, not analysing them or trying to make sense of them. There are many techniques that will help you to achieve this, including my own 'Fish Tank' technique which I explained in a previous chapter. The technique used is not important as long as you are able to observe your thoughts without interference. With practice you will be able to free yourself from uncontrolled thought and take complete charge of your mind, thinking what you want when you want.

Question your beliefs and opinions

Question each and every belief and opinion you have. Can your beliefs and opinions be proved or disproved? Don't mistake a strong belief for proof. You may believe strongly in the existence of fairies or little green men from Mars, but if you cannot prove it absolutely 100% then let it go. Beliefs and opinions can be seriously limiting and harmful to your happiness, stress levels, health and life.

Surrender to all that is

The surrendering sounds like a difficult step, but it is actually one of the easiest steps to take once you have achieved the first two steps. Once your mind is clear of uncontrolled thought and free from limiting beliefs and opinions, you are free to just let go and accept all and everything around you. Surrendering doesn't mean that you like, support, agree or disagree with anything, just that you accept that things are the way they are. It doesn't mean that you cannot try to change things, just that you accept them as they are now.

Just be

Finding time to just be is more about the mental rather than the physical. Just being is a state of mind that can exist alongside the physical tasks of everyday life. It's the combination and accumulation of the previous three steps. Its a complete stillness of the mind free from thought (controlled or uncontrolled), beliefs and opinions.

Be happy

Why would you want to be anything else? Happiness is the key to everything and can only ever be total and complete when experienced from within. Happiness does not come from the outside by way of possessions, but from within by way of acceptance. Think about the things that make you happy now and you will realise that the happiness comes from the way those things make you feel. You are happy because you have a total acceptance of them. As soon as you stop accepting them you are no longer happy. You now have a choice to accept everything and be happy always.

When life tries to drag you into
its problems tell yourself
'Not my circus, not my Monkeys'